PARENTING
THROUGH
THE RANKS

T0205041

Because of the dynamic nature of the Internet, web addresses or links contained in this book may have been changed since publication and may no longer be valid. The content of this book and all expressed opinions are those of the author. The author is solely responsible for all content included herein.

PARENTING
THROUGH
THE RANKS

HOW TO RAISE
SUCCESSFUL SCOUTS

DAVID HARAKAL

FALCON®

Essex, Connecticut

An imprint of The Globe Pequot Publishing Group, Inc.
64 South Main Street
Essex, CT 06426
www.globepequot.com

Falcon and FalconGuides are registered trademarks and Make Adventure Your Story is a trademark of The Globe Pequot Publishing Group, Inc.

Distributed by NATIONAL BOOK NETWORK

Cover design by Ruth Gunadi @ elQue.design | 99Designs
Interior layout by Kathy Lee
Edited by Siobhan Gallagher
Proofread by Abbey McLaughlin

British Library Cataloguing in Publication Information available

Library of Congress Control Number: 2023909302

ISBN 9781493088508 (paperback) | ISBN 9781493088515 (ebook)

∞™ The paper used in this publication meets the minimum requirements of American National Standard for Information Sciences—Permanence of Paper for Printed Library Materials, ANSI/NISO Z39.48-1992.

TABLE OF CONTENTS

CONTENTS

CONTENTS

ACKNOWLEDGMENTS

Thank you to all the Scouters who taught me Scouting and joined my wife and children in refining my parenting.

Particular thanks to Bill Bryson, Ron Luke, Bob Oatman, and Johanna van der Zwan for their valuable advice when reviewing my manuscript, and my sister, Cora, for her review and editing.

Our children, Callie and Timothy, survived my parenting blunders— and ended up amazing.

My long-suffering wife endured and gently corrected me. I love you, Suzanne, and thank you for your partnership in raising our two successful Scouts.

PREFACE

*The only thing necessary for the triumph of evil
is for good men to do nothing.*

— EDMUND BURKE

*The spirit is there in every boy;
it has to be discovered and brought to light.*

— ROBERT BADEN-POWELL

I needed this book when I was a Scout dad. Had it existed, and had I the humility to follow the advice it contains, my children's Scouting experiences would have been more meaningful, my relationship with them would have been deeper and richer, and I would have been a more thoughtful husband.

"Do not make the same mistakes—make new ones!" was my signature phrase when I conducted training courses. Scouting reflects that sentiment. So should parenting. Scouting, Scouts, and Scouters improved how I raised my children. I wrote this book for you to benefit from what I learned.

Parents, I would be unfaithful to the Scout Law if I did not provide you the benefit of my hard-won wisdom. I spent over twenty years raising a daughter and a son, including a dozen as a Scout parent. Why should you repeat the errors I made or saw others make? Improve on what I did well and what better parents taught me. Then go make new mistakes and learn from them (and e-mail them to me so I can add them to future revisions)!

Scouting teaches respect for others, leadership, and citizenship. These should apply to the family first. I loved our children's teen years. Yes, you read that correctly. We butted heads at times as a strong-willed parent raising strong-willed children, but we maintained mutual respect and enjoyed relatively open dialogue. That is the other reason I wrote this book. I want to help other parents enjoy parenting, not suffer through it— to delight in their children, not tolerate them. Teen years characterized by conflict are not inevitable—they are a joint effort created over time.

Your Scout needs you to be the best parent you can be to enable him or her to become the best person they can be. I hope this book will help.

David Harakal
August 2023

CHAPTER ONE

SCOUT PARENT— THIS BOOK IS FOR YOU

An invaluable step in character training is to put responsibility on the individual.

— ROBERT BADEN-POWELL

Welcome to the adventure of a lifetime.[1]

— MICHAEL B. SURBAUGH,
CHIEF SCOUT EXECUTIVE,
BOY SCOUTS OF AMERICA®

Scouting rises within you and inspires you to put forth your best.

— JULIETTE GORDON LOW, FOUNDER,
GIRL SCOUTS OF THE USA

---

1. From the 2019 edition of the Scouts BSA Handbook.

Walk worthy.

– TRAIL LIFE USA MOTTO

American Heritage Girls love to serve.

– PATTY GARIBAY, FOUNDER

If you want your child to succeed in Scouts, desire mutual respect during their adolescent and teen years borne out of a rich relationship, and are willing to adapt your parenting style to meet changing needs as he or she matures, then this is the book for you. The advice I offer aligns with Scout ages, stages, and advancement goals to prepare your son or daughter to thrive in Scouts, in school, and in life.

Scouting America, Girl Scouts of the USA, Trail Life USA, American Heritage Girls, the World Organization of the Scout Movement, and World Association of Girl Guides and Girl Scouts are the best youth leadership and character development programs in the world. Robert Baden-Powell founded the Scouting movement in 1907 to "[t]ry and leave this world a little better than you found it." This book will help you guide your child to this end.

Future chapters reflect the structure of the Scouting America program. If I tried to reflect every Scouting organization in each detail, my main points would be overshadowed by the distraction of mapping among programs and result in a thick tome, cumbersome to read. I have intentionally kept this book short by limiting variables and stories, so if you have questions, e-mail them to me at Scouting@DHarakalAuthor.org. Visit my website, DHarakalAuthor.org, for answers and additional materials.

I use the *fleur-de-lis* motif throughout this book as representative of the 50-million-strong World Scouting movement, of which Scouting America is a charter member and active participant, and because it was the symbol the founder incorporated into Scouting from its earliest days.

(In 1910, Baden-Powell and his sister, Agnes, founded the Girl Guide Association, which evolved into the World Association of Girl Guides and Girl Scouts, of which Girl Scouts USA is a part.)

Approximate age and stage equivalencies for the different Scouting organizations are listed in a footnote on the first page of each chapter.

DISCLAIMER

None of the Scouting organizations asked me to write this book nor had any influence over it. No representatives reviewed this book in an official capacity. All opinions are mine.

As a Scout parent and/or volunteer, you must understand the policies of your Scouting organization, which change over time to protect you and your child. At publication, nothing in this guide conflicts with any published Scouting policy to my knowledge. If you discover any discrepancies, please notify me at Scouting@DHarakalAuthor.org and I will make corrections.

This does not mean I wrote in a vacuum. I am thankful to several Scouters with successful Scouts and adult children who reviewed my manuscript. I welcome your feedback.

All web links were correct at publication. If you find one in error, please send me the updated link and I will correct it in future copies.

CHAPTER TWO

WHY YOU NEED TO READ THIS BOOK

Affirming words from moms and dads are like light switches.
Speak a word of affirmation at the right moment in a child's life
and it's like lighting up a whole roomful of possibilities.

– GARY SMALLEY

The sport in Scouting is to find the good in every boy and develop it.

– ROBERT BADEN-POWELL

Is it your child's goal to become an Eagle Scout? Eagle is a noble achievement and impressive accomplishment fewer than 0.3% of American teenagers earn. But is that goal sufficient? Have you prepared your child for life after Scouts? They need more than advancement to build the moral stamina and depth of character necessary to endure for a lifetime. If your son or daughter becomes an Eagle Scout yet your relationship deteriorates, you both lose.

If the amount of your attention your child receives from you directly correlates to the accolades or correction they receive from others, please read this book.

If your Scout progresses only because of your threats or bribes, it is time to stop and consider whose dreams they are chasing. You need this book.

Are you content with your relationship with your child? Is your child content? If you answered yes to either or both, subsequent life stages, different Scouting ranks, and other children will require different parenting skills and techniques. Not one of us is a perfect parent without room for improvement. This book is for you.

There are many books, websites, and blogs to teach you about Scout programs. If you master Scouting knowledge but not how to shepherd your child, they will advance but not reach their full life potential. Use this book, combined with Scouts, to help you draw out your son or daughter's unique spirit through each phase of Scouting, to challenge and guide you to develop mutual respect, and to equip you to earn your Scout's adulation.

This guide provides answers to questions like:

- ⚜ How should my Scout define success?
- ⚜ How do I define success for my Scout?
- ⚜ Should I define success for my Scout?
- ⚜ How do I help my child advance, to learn from failure and success?
- ⚜ How much should I push?
- ⚜ What fears might my child experience, and how do I help them overcome those concerns?

- ♣ How can I help my child fit in and make new friends?

- ♣ How do I talk to my teenager?

- ♣ How do I get my teenager to talk to me?

- ♣ How do I incorporate Scouting into a holistic program of moral and character development?

The most often repeated and highest impact parental error I have seen in Scouting (and in sports and academics) is one my Scout showed me in myself—Scouting *through* your child, not *for* your child. My son, in wisdom beyond his years, exposed my flawed parenting when I pushed him toward a campout he was not ready to attend. He said, "Dad, this is *Boy* Scouts, not Man Scouts." Ouch!

It is never too late to adjust how you parent. Your children may have worn you down and left you feeling hopeless. Your children might be models of character and respect such that their teachers ask other parents to talk to you for advice. Wherever you fall on that spectrum, this book can help you. I share successful parenting practices I learned from others, from my own successes and failures, and what I wish I had known when I was parenting my Scouts.

If you are easily offended or too prideful to admit your mistakes and change, let this book challenge you. Your child needs you to be their role model. Do you keep yourself morally straight? Would your child agree that you do right when others do not and avoid wrong though others succumb? (Ask them!) Do you show respect for others, including those with whom you disagree? How you parent must change as your child moves through life stages, Scouting and otherwise.

Scouting develops a child's ability to set and meet goals, to lead and be led by others, and master skills few non-Scouting youth learn—if you do not get in the way. Your Scout will learn how to challenge peers, hold them to a high standard, encourage them, and share hard truths. You need to model this. Parenting is hard. You do not need someone pandering to your feelings to the detriment of your child's potential, so I do not hold back. My measure for this book's success is the degree to which it helps you become the parent your Scout needs.

I made some good parenting decisions. Many were redeemed bad decisions. I was prideful and self-righteous. God changed my heart while our children were in high school. People really can change. I did.

If your parenting style needs to change, change it now. It gets harder to undo the damage done the longer you put it off. Do not wait until your relationship deteriorates to the point where only a miracle could revive it.

The following pages may imply I was Super Dad, half of the Parenting Incredibles. No. They do not exist. We were not and are not. Your child, like ours, has more grace for you than you have for yourself. Make mistakes, make apologies, make amends, and make progress toward becoming a parent worthy of your child's respect. Help guide them to grow into the best man or woman they can be. They follow your lead, so lead well.

Your child came to you without an instruction manual. It is difficult to raise a child as society tries to undermine your authority. I hope this book helps you to navigate the confusing and sometimes dangerous road ahead, and that you arrive at your destination: a joyful relationship with your child.

CHAPTER THREE

MY QUALIFICATIONS

Correcting bad habits cannot be done by forbidding or punishment.

– ROBERT BADEN-POWELL

Train up a child in the way he should go, and when he is old,
he will not depart from it.

– PROVERBS 22:6 *(NKJV)*

Who am I to give you advice?

My Scouting experience as an average Scout who never made it past Second Class in a run-of-the-mill troop does not qualify me to write this book. Raising an Eagle Scout and a Venturing crew president who were part of exceptional units in stellar districts and a supportive council taught me Scouting and improved my parenting. This was my school of hard knocks, my on-the-job training.

I am not a perfect parent writing a book to tell you how to raise your child. Quite the contrary. Any honest dad or mom would question their qualifications to give child-rearing advice. People ask me, "What did you do? Your children are amazing! What is your secret?"

How do I answer?

"First, there are no guarantees. We did our best and strove to learn, adapt, and improve, and something in that mix worked. Second, God gave us intelligent children with incredible abilities, and we did not do too much to mess those up."

Your child has unique abilities and talents. Part of your parenting job is to help him or her discover and refine them.

MY BACKGROUND

Scouting: I was the senior patrol leader (SPL) of a tiny troop when I was only a Second Class Scout. That is where I peaked. Not a stellar reference point. But as a Scouter,[2] my history is more robust. I was a Tiger Cub coach back when that was the youngest rank, an assistant den leader, Webelos den leader, assistant Scoutmaster, assistant Venturing crew advisor, district camping chair, troop and district advancement chair, unit commissioner, and a merit badge counselor for over a dozen different merit badges (taught many times, in different settings). I developed and led a Webelos-Scout-to-Scouts-BSA transition program and was a National Youth Leadership Training course director, among several other titled and non-titled roles. The council awarded me a Vale la Pena! service award and a Silver Beaver Award, and I received a Gold Level President's Volunteer Service Award three times.

Professional Career: I spent over thirty years in corporate America. For twenty-one of those, I worked at IBM, where I developed and led the pricing integration practice for software mergers and acquisitions. After

---

2. For this book, I use the term "Scouter" to refer to a Scout parent or any other adult who works with Scouts.

IBM, I re-engineered business models for several other $1 billion companies, private and public.

Other Tidbits: I started four Toastmasters clubs, created a fine arts booster for our children's school, served as a deacon and an elder at a large church, was an Advisory Board member for the University of Texas at Austin Parents Association, and wrote an update to John Bunyan's classic allegory, which I entitled *The Pilgrim's Progress for the 21st Century*.

Marriage: My wife and I have been married thirty-four years and raised our children as a team. God used our differences to create checks and balances in our parenting. We currently care for Christians living cross-culturally from our home in the Middle East/North Africa region.

OUR SCOUTS

The most credible evidence I can offer you is that we parented two children into healthy adulthood.

Our married daughter is a neonatology fellow at Washington University in Saint Louis, Missouri. In high school, she was a Venturing crew president (back when girls were not part of Boy Scouts) who became a Red Cross instructor at sixteen years old, and presented and/or created CPR and first-aid training programs for Girl Scout troops, Scouts BSA troops, a Webelos summer camp, Scout parents, and leaders. One of the young Girl Scouts she trained used the skills she learned to save another child's life.

Our married son is a regional director who trains people for the mission field. He is an Eagle Scout with two silver palms, an Order of the Arrow Vigil Honor member, was SPL for a troop with about one hundred Scouts, a National Youth Leadership Training SPL, a junior assistant Scoutmaster, earned a Presidential Gold Service Award, and led a Philmont expedition to name a few of his Scouting accomplishments.

He will tell you that Scouts was a significant factor in developing the skills needed to lead teams, equip those who report to him and others, and facilitate change in his organization.

I share this not to boast but to establish credibility. I would like to fully claim credit for our children's success, but that would be foolish. God trusted us to shepherd the gifts He gave them.

CHAPTER FOUR

WHAT IS SCOUTING?

We never fail when we try to do our duty.
We always fail when we neglect to do it.

— ROBERT BADEN-POWELL

In all of this, it is the spirit that matters.
Our Scout law and Promise, when we really put them into practice,
take away all occasion for wars and strife among nations.

— ROBERT BADEN-POWELL

To support your Scout and Scouting, it is important for you to know what your child's program espouses. At the time of publication, these statements from www.scouting.org will help you understand the aims and methods used in Scouting America. Other programs follow similar principles to greater or lesser degrees.

MISSION

The mission of Scouting America is to prepare young people to make ethical and moral choices over their lifetimes by instilling in them the values of the Scout Oath and Law.

VISION

Scouting America will prepare every eligible youth in America to become a responsible, participating citizen and leader who is guided by the Scout Oath and Law.

VALUE OF SCOUTING

Discovery is at the heart of Scouting. Whether it's a campout, derby car race, or hike on a trail, we believe every adventure helps us uncover a little more about ourselves. We build the foundations for humility and com-passion—strengthening character through actions—to prepare youth for a lifetime of leadership.

SCOUT OATH

On my honor, I will do my best to do my duty to God and my country and to obey the Scout Law; to help other people at all times; to keep myself physically strong, mentally awake, and morally straight.

SCOUT LAW

A Scout is trustworthy, loyal, helpful, friendly, courteous, kind, obedient, cheerful, thrifty, brave, clean, and reverent.

Prepared. For Life.

Scouting teaches youth to confront any challenge with whole hearts and clear minds—to live their lives without regret, never back down, and do their very best!

Scouting's Bottom Line[3]

What happens to a Scout? For every 100 children who join Scouting, records indicate that:

- *Rarely* will one be brought before the juvenile court system;
- 4 will become Eagle Scouts;
- 17 will become future Scout volunteers;
- 12 will have their first contact with a church;
- 1 will enter the clergy;
- 5 will earn their church award;
- 18 will develop a hobby that will last through their adult life;
- 8 will enter a vocation that was learned through the merit badge system;
- 1 will use his Scouting skills to save his own life; and
- 1 will use his Scouting skills to save the life of another person.

---

3. www.usscouts.org/usscouts/eagle/bottomline.asp, 2007.

PARENTING THROUGH THE RANKS

Scouting's alumni record is equally impressive. A recent nationwide survey of high schools revealed the following information:

- 85% of student council presidents were Scouts;
- 89% of senior class presidents were Scouts;
- 80% of junior class presidents were Scouts;
- 75% of school publication editors were Scouts; and
- 71% of football captains were Scouts.

Scouts also account for:

- 64% of Air Force Academy graduates;
- 68% of West Point graduates;
- 70% of Annapolis graduates;
- 72% of Rhodes Scholars;
- 85% of FBI agents; and
- 26 of the first 29 astronauts, including the first man to walk on the moon and the entire Apollo 13 crew.

CHAPTER FIVE

SCOUT PARENTING FOUNDATIONS

Children are not a distraction from more important work.
They are the most important work.

— C. S. Lewis

See things from the boy's point of view.

— Robert Baden-Powell

One of the greatest gifts you can give to your Scout is Scouting with them. How directly will vary based on their stage in Scouts, but involving yourself in their world—Scouting and otherwise—will establish a foundation on which to build a strong relationship of mutual respect.

Encourage, challenge, equip, empower, and support your child, then celebrate their successes with them. But these successes must be theirs.

Robert Baden-Powell said, "When you want a thing done, 'Don't do it yourself' is a good motto for Scoutmasters."[4] It is also a good motto

---

4. *Boy Scouts of America: Order of the Arrow,* oa-bsa.org/history/lord-baden-powell.

for parents. My derivation of that principle is: "Do nothing for children that they can do alone or with the help of peers." Your child's ability will change over time, and you must understand their intellectual, physical, and emotional capacities to avoid expecting too much—or too little. Adherence to this approach ensures your Scout celebrates their successes, not yours.

What can your child do alone or with the help of peers? What are reasonable expectations? Proverbs 22:6 is familiar to most people, regardless of religious conviction, and it provides a useful framework to determine your child's distinct aptitudes and to understand what they can do on their own or with the help of peers. It says, "Train up a child in the way he should go, and when he is old, he will not depart from it." (NKJV) Some parents read this as: "Direct your child into the person you want them to be." There is an element of that perspective, but a parent must first learn their child's distinct attributes, or "bent," to help them use their aptitudes to become the person God designed them to be. Scouting aids that process through activities that encourage your child to explore different interests. Scouts has helped many find new hobbies, passions, and even careers. For our daughter, a Venturing crew focused on first aid refined and fueled her desire to become a physician.

Scouting America has developed an effective tool to teach your Scout new skills called the EDGE Method: Explain, Demonstrate, Guide, and Enable. For more details, read the article linked in the footnote from *Scouting Magazine*.[5] All four steps are important. Do not sell your Scout short by omitting one of them. Employ the EDGE Method at home as well.

Teach in times of non-conflict. An upset child is not ready to sit down for a lengthy conversation. Address the immediate issue, but "do not pro-

---

5. Bryan Wendell, "The Teaching EDGE: The Best way to Teach Someone a New Skill," *Aaron on Scouting*, May 5, 2017, blog.scoutingmagazine.org/2017/05/05/living-on-the-edge-this-is-the-correct-way-to-teach-someone-a-skill.

voke your children, lest they become discouraged."[6] When you have both calmed down, discuss the incident and then teach.

How to Start Scouting

Set your child up for success with a good start. To begin your child's Scouting journey, find a Cub Scout pack, a Scouts BSA troop, a Venturing crew, or a Sea Scout ship that fits their goals and your family's priorities.[7] Convenience is helpful, but value alignment is vital.

Scouting organizations have gone to great lengths to protect your child, so that Scouting offers an amazing opportunity for your child to learn leadership from positive male and female role models.

Do not rely on hearsay in your search for the right unit. Visit different packs, troops, crews, or ships. Talk to committee members and parents. Observe how other Scouts interact with your child—are they welcomed, shunned, or ignored? Ask the questions listed in the appendices at the end of this book.

Your Cub Scout will more quickly integrate into a pack with other families from their school or religious institution where they have existing friendships. In Scouts BSA, Venturing, or Sea Scouts, discuss priorities—your child has to be involved in the decision. It is *your Scout's* troop. Is your child's highest priority to become an Eagle Scout? Is high adventure their passion? Does the unit support your family's faith? Does your older Scout need a new friend group or to join in with existing friends? Make sure you each agree with the unit's methods, goals, and principles. Use the questions in the appendices as your guide.

When you visit a Cub Scout pack, parents run the meetings, so it should look pretty organized. But with Scouts BSA, Venturing, and Sea

---

6. Colossians 3:31, Holy Bible, English Standard Version.

7. If you are not sure what these terms mean, visit www.scouting.org to review the different programs that Scouting America offers.

Scouts, the Scouts are in charge. You are visiting a leadership incubator. Is the meeting seamless, smooth, and efficient? That could be a warning sign that parents are leading more than Scouts. (Note: If your child is too old for Cub Scouts and interested in earning their Eagle, find a Scouting America troop. Scouts must earn their First Class rank in a troop before pursuing their Eagle rank in a Venturing crew or Sea Scouts ship.)

If possible, go a step further and join a campout. Baden-Powell said, "A week of camp life is worth six months of theoretical teaching in the meeting room." It is also the best place to learn how a unit operates.

In college, I visited a leadership development center in the countryside near Yorkshire, England. For one exercise, we repaired a dry-fit stone wall with no experience or instruction. We then hiked in the rain, including overnight in a tent, with only maps of ancient stone walls for a guide. The unfamiliar environments, unexpected circumstances, and lack of control over weather found outdoors tests leaders of all ages and experience levels. In Scouting, weekend campouts provide the ideal peek into a unit in action so you can watch the leadership incubator in its native environment, visit with parents around the campfire, and give your son or daughter time to see if the unit fits.

Once your child has joined, get trained.

You may be thinking, "Wait, that is for Scout leaders, not me. Who has time for that?" Do not let training worries deter you. Youth Protection Training (YPT) is required for any parent who wants to help lead or camp, but every parent should take it. Start there. It will comfort you to learn the lengths to which Scouting America goes to protect you both. Future chapters will provide more specific training details to benefit you, your child, and your Scout's unit as you discover the methods behind the madness and why the unit operates the way it does. Much training is available online, although I recommend attending in person when possible for the valuable connections and lifelong friendships you will develop.

If you read this book for help with an older Scout, at least scan the chapters written for parenting younger Scouts as later chapters build on them.

EVALUATE YOUR PARENTING

You are ready to jump into Scouting. You want to help your child. Will how you are currently parenting lead to the happiness and emotional health your Scout needs to succeed? You can answer that question by assessing your parenting style through a warmth/discipline grid. Research confirms that children raised by authoritative (not authoritarian) parents who create a high warmth/high discipline environment see the best life outcomes.[8] From a child's point of view, I would summarize the authoritative parent as: "I never doubt my mom and dad love me, and because of their love, they set and enforce rules to protect me." These children are more open to positive reinforcement and correction because of the mutual respect and unconditional love they feel.

Enter your child's world, learn who they are, open a door for them to share their fears and concerns, to seek your advice, and to grow closer to you. Zig Ziglar said, "To a child, love is spelled T-I-M-E." This is high warmth/love. Take to heart what Theodore Roosevelt is credited with saying: "Nobody cares how much you know until they know how much you care." Set aside dedicated time to discuss how you see your Scout use their talents and explore their passions, or discover them together.

If you use this time to berate your child for a mistake or character flaw you want to correct rather than ask questions and listen, you will shut down discussion and set up a battle of wills. Instead, prepare for amazing

---

8. Conville, Nicola, "There are FOUR parenting styles but THIS one raises more successful kids," *Practical Parenting*, July 2, 2019, www.practicalparenting.com.au/four-parenting-styles-but-this-one-raises-more-successful-kids.

teenage years by knowing your child and letting them know you (with age-appropriate boundaries). You are their parent, not their friend.

My wife and I attended an intensive marriage counseling retreat where each participant created a genogram and shared it with the group. (The genograms mapped family history from birth through high school.) Many of the participants did not feel known by their parents who did not enter their world, and they brought the resulting painful emotional baggage into their marriages. Do not do that to your son or daughter.

As your child matures, it is healthy and beneficial for your direct involvement to decrease. You should expect some degree of distancing during their teen years if you are teaching them how to succeed without you. You must teach them how to make well-informed decisions. When your teenager pulls away, even though you show them unconditional love, ask open-ended questions and actively listen; they still need you—be available to talk when they are ready.[9]

When your son or daughter seeks your counsel, it is a sign that your relationship is on firm ground and that they trust you to have their best interest at heart, even when they disagree and ignore you.

If your goal is to prevent your child's growth, hinder the mission, vision, aims, and methods of Scouting,[10] and render the EDGE Method ineffective, practice helicopter parenting. Your constant presence might seem like high warmth/love to you because you see yourself as always being there for your child, but what your child sees is a lack of trust. This parent lives through their child's accolades and thus robs the Scout from claiming that success as their own. Your Scout will learn powerful lessons from the natural consequences of non-catastrophic failure. Do not under-

---

9. "Active listening with pre-teens and teenagers," *Raising Children.net, The Australian Parenting Website*, Sept. 7, 2021, raisingchildren.net.au/pre-teens/communicating-relationships /communicating/active-listening.

10. Troopleader.scouting.org/scoutings-aims-and-methods.

mine this teacher. Are you a helicopter parent? Your friends may not tell you, but WebMD will.[11]

The second-best way to undermine Scouting's benefits is to practice drop-off parenting. For this misguided parent, BSA, Scouting America's previous name, is an acronym for "Babysitters of America." You leave your child at Scouts or delegate that responsibility to someone else so you can pursue your hobby or go back to work. You might attend a unit meeting, blue and gold banquet, or court of honor if you have nothing better to do, but cannot imagine a weekend without the comforts of home. Few would recognize you if you showed up at a Scouting event. Your view of "supporting the unit" is paying dues and, if you have extra funds not earmarked for something you want, an occasional donation to Friends of Scouting.[12]

I do not mean to minimize a single parent's struggle, the demands on parents with multiple children and/or more than one job, or a parent whose work schedule unavoidably conflicts with Scouts. Parents also show commitment when they help with advancement at home, join in Scout activities when possible, and help the unit remotely (including database management, coordinating awards to order from your Scout shop, or other organizational support).

Every parent and adult leader should model servant leadership and develop or expand a heart for others. "Humility is not thinking less of yourself but thinking of yourself less."[13] Does your life reflect this sentiment from C. S. Lewis? If not, you will not see it reflected in your child's life either. Demonstrate this in the way you serve other adults in the troop. Support leaders at home and at meetings, even if only by thanking them when you pick up or drop off your Scout. Do not undermine unit leaders

---

11. Brennan, Dan, "7 Signs You Might Be a Helicopter Parent," *Grow by WebMD,* Nov. 23, 2022, www.webmd.com/parenting/ss/slideshow-helicopter-parent.

12. Bryan Wendell, "What is Friends of Scouting," *Aaron on Scouting,* October 16, 2015, blog.scoutingmagazine.org/2015/10/16/what-is-friends-of-scouting.

13. Clive Staples Lewis, paraphrased by Rick Warren in *The Purpose Driven Life*, Book III, Chapter 8. Adapted from a series of BBC Radio talks between 1942 and 1944.

by speaking ill of them in their absence. If you have a concern, discuss it with the person directly, honorably, and humbly. "Seek not so much to be understood as to understand."[14]

CONSISTENCY

Consistency has two core elements important for a happy household. First, parents must agree how to parent. You will have subtle differences in how you respond and interact with your children, but you must have the same parenting strategy, rules, and consequences. A child who asks one parent a question and does not receive the answer they want, then asks the other, commits a serious infraction that warrants a serious punishment. But if parents do not agree on parenting strategies and create a chaotic environment for their child that fosters such behavior, that is a parenting failure. Mom and Dad, you must find common ground on how you parent. If you find yourselves at an impasse, consider engaging a counselor, spiritual leader, or mentor to help you.

The second element of consistency is holding the line when you are tired or worn down. Your "yes" must be "yes," and your "no" must be "no." If you allow your child to berate you with whining until you submit to their wishes, you will create a whiny, pestering child. Begging, pestering, and delaying is disobedience and requires a related consequence. For example, if it is bedtime and your child pesters you for more time, they might go to bed fifteen minutes earlier for the next few nights.

Are there exceptions? Yes, especially for new information offered in humility ahead of the infraction. Say your teen's curfew is ten o'clock on weeknights. Your child, who is conscientious about compliance, calls you at 9:45 to tell you that their friend ordered pizza for dinner but delivery was late and it just arrived. In this case, consider a reasonable extension

---

14. *The Prayer of St. Francis*, St. Francis of Assisi.

together, then hold to that new time. If your child arrives home at 10:30 and tells you their pizza was late, this is a violation of their curfew and requires a consequence. Communication in advance is the difference.

Do rules never change? Must rules be the same for every child? No and no. How you parent must change as your child matures and earns new privileges commensurate with new responsibilities. Teenage rules must be different from ten-year-old expectations. Even if you have ten-year-old twins, you might have slightly different rules based on their personalities and needs, but the differences must be fair and based on the differences in your child. This is a difficult but important balance. No one told you parenting would be easy, did they? If so, they lied.

EXPERIENTIAL LEARNING TOOLS

Scouts must be a safe place to fail. Home, more so. If your Scout is not free to try and fail with you, start now. Thomas J. Watson, IBM's first chairman and CEO, said, "Failure is a teacher; a harsh one, but the best." You can buffer some of that harshness and increase your child's learning potential if they have your unconditional love at all times, but particularly as they try new activities and make mistakes.

Deep mutual trust in your relationship opens your son or daughter to learn from you. Try the Oreo cookie model—sandwich one part of correction between two parts of praise. This shows them you recognize what they did well and that your focus is not solely on their failings. It works in all Scouting phases, outside of Scouts, and with adults.

Use Scout traditions and training to teach through successes and failures. After events, especially campouts, Scout leaders ask the Scouts of any age to share their "thorns, roses, and buds." A thorn is an experience or activity that went awry or was unpleasant.. A rose is a pleasant memory or a successful adventure. A bud is an idea for the future. Try it at home, especially if you cannot attend a unit outing. This exercise will help both of you better prepare for future events and grow as leaders when you observe how others respond to unexpected events. Roses may highlight the benefits of careful planning while thorns could reflect the opposite. Consider doing this over ice cream, at a favorite restaurant, on a walk, or any place special to your child. Make it a routine you both enjoy. Connect while the memories are fresh. Focus on growing closer to your son or daughter, learning together, not interrogation.

Start, Stop, Continue (SSC) is another tool employed with troops, crews, or ships. Scouts discuss what they think they should Start doing, Stop doing, or Continue doing, often as part of a planning meeting or when training new youth leaders. Practice this at home to teach your Scout how to distinguish good from bad leadership, develop their own leadership style, and discuss how they can contribute as a team member.

These tools help you stay in touch with your child as their world changes and to dream with them as their dreams change. Or, as Baden-Powell said, "See things from the [child]'s point of view." The astute parent listens for fears and frustrations, which your son or daughter may not even realize they have. Enjoy a deeper relationship through your focused attention and genuine interest without condemnation.

And remember to celebrate the roses!

FAMILY DYNAMICS

As you read further, you will notice the context of the "traditional nuclear family." I recognize that family structures vary, but incorporating every dynamic would make this book too long. To keep it succinct, I have written from the perspective of my own situation: father and mother with a child or children. Extensive research reveals the strong, positive impact committed parents have on their children.[15] The Scouting America website says: "Whether a Cub Scout lives with two parents or one, a foster family, or other relatives, their family is an important part of Cub Scouting."[16] Although written for Cub Scouts, this statement is true for all Scouts, though in different ways and to different degrees.

This book's guidance applies almost universally, though I recognize the challenge will be greater in some family dynamics than in others. Be the parent your child needs to equip him or her to be "physically strong, mentally awake, and morally straight."[17] (If you have specific questions about parenting in different family settings, please e-mail me.)

For Scouts in two-parent households, who makes the better Scouter, Mom or Dad? Ideally, the same-sex parent (more on the rationale later). Some families do not have that choice. For a single parent, or when the same-sex parent cannot take an active role in their child's life, Scouting is an excellent opportunity for boys to learn from positive male role models and girls to learn from positive female role models. In units where dads lead boys, all dads and sons teach and learn from each other. The same is true for female Scout units. This reinforces the importance of selecting a unit that aligns with your family's values—your child will learn from everyone there.

In some families, neither parent can be involved. If this is not you, find out how to support that family (rides to or from meetings, outings, clothing or gear, etc.). My son and I volunteered with an inner-city district where parental involvement was almost nonexistent. We had Scouters with grown children, plus single men and women with Scouting experience, step in to lead.

---

15. Jane Anderson, "ACP position paper: The impact of family structure on the health of children: Effects of divorce," *The Linacre Quarterly 81,* Catholic Medical Association, 2014, www.ncbi.nlm.nih.gov/pmc/articles/PMC4240051/pdf/lnq-81-378.pdf.

16. www.scouting.org/programs/cub-scouts/aims-and-methods.

17. From the Scout Oath.

Please do not misinterpret this section. I do not advocate that only one parent be active in Scouts. I made that mistake much to the detriment of our children and my wife. Your child needs both of you; each of you must lead them, and you should both be involved, albeit to different degrees. Some Scouts do succeed without parental support, but they are the exceptions.

Healthy parent-child relationships flourish only when your child respects you. They need parents, not live-in adult friends. If you do not teach them, someone else will.

Mom and Dad, build each other up. Hold each other accountable. You are each important for your child's healthy development. Undermine each other, criticize the other, find fault with your spouse or ex-spouse, and you add stress and uncertainty to your child's life, sometimes to a debilitating degree. They need stability at home to navigate a healthy path to maturity. Divorce or an unhealthy marriage does not excuse you from being the best parent you can be for your child or children. Do not blame others for your mistakes.

Fathers, do not underestimate your influence on your child's social, emotional, academic, and spiritual development during *every* stage of life. I have known too many dads who are good financial providers, yet meet no relational needs and who prioritize their free time for personal hobbies over family. Do not cede your role to someone else. Fatherlessness has a devastating effect on the household and society.[18] Scouting provides a ready-made environment for a father to be involved with his children, within and outside of the unit.

I simplified this book by not addressing all child dynamics. Some children are ready and eager to comply while others seem to pick a fight at every word. My advice applies to both, with one more readily accepting

---

18. Jack Brewer, "Fatherlessness and Its Effects on American Society," *AFPI (America First Policy Institute)*, February 15, 2022, assets.americafirstpolicy.com/assets/uploads/files/Fatherhood_Research_Paper_V2.pdf.

than the other. I also do not address learning difficulties, developmental challenges, or medical maladies. These complicate parenting, but you will still find helpful guidance in this book.

There are excellent books, podcasts, and other resources available to help you parent your child. (I list my favorite parenting books in the "Additional Resources" chapter.) None of these can, or should, replace your religion's holy book(s), which I encourage you to read as a family. Your children need to see you study the tenets of your faith, learn from them, and rely on them in your life.

CHAPTER SIX

CUB SCOUTS—LION TO WEBELOS

Play is often talked about as if it were a relief from serious learning.
But for children, play is serious learning.
Play is really the work of childhood.

— Fred Rogers

Nobody is too small to do a good turn, even if it is only to smile.

— Robert Baden-Powell

If your child starts Scouting as a Lion Cub,[19] **you only have about ten years of focused attention left.** Let that sink in. By the time your Scout reaches the middle-teen years, friends will command a greater share of their focus. Invest now in your future teenager.

You are your Cub Scout's trusted guide. Your child wants to be like you. I hope that intimidates you. It intimidated me.

---

19. CUB SCOUTS: Lion to Webelos; Ages 5–10 years/Kindergarten–4th Grade; GIRL SCOUTS: Daisy, Brownie; TRAIL LIFE: Woodlands Trail; SCOUTS: Beaver, Cub; GUIDES: Rainbow; AMERICAN HERITAGE GIRLS: Pathfinder, Tenderheart.

Attend meetings and outings together as often as possible. Encourage your Scout to try every activity. Cubs learn through parental involvement, engaging games, and enjoyable activities geared to their age. Scouts is fun but intentional. As Baden-Powell said: "Scouting is a game with a purpose." Your parenting also needs some fun in it. Your Scout should look forward to their time working on advancement and awards with you. The outcome? They will develop skills and grow in confidence as you build a foundation of trust and mutual respect.

Coach, cheerlead, partner in learning, and watch your child thrive. Help during activities, but do nothing for your Scout that they can do for themselves or with help from peers. Follow the EDGE Method, not the do-it-for-your-Scout method. Encourage them to teach friends and family.

Begin a habit of asking questions to learn about your child and show interest in their Scouting program. Give them your undivided attention when they answer.

Prepare Your Child for Cub Scouts

You are your child's hero, beloved Mom or Dad. He or she will follow where you lead. Enter your child's world to help them grow and mature. Interact at their physical and mental level. Kneel or sit so you can work on new challenges together, eye to eye. Your presence in their world will carry relational benefits throughout their life and build a relationship to make obedience easier for you both.

Your child needs you to establish and enforce boundaries and rules in an atmosphere of love and acceptance. Their default must be immediate compliance when you give direction ("first-time obedience") to be prepared for emergencies possible on campouts or other outings. Counting to three and other threats teach deferred compliance, which is noncompliance, and can be dangerous for your Scout.

It is best to develop patterns of compliance prior to kindergarten, starting at birth.[20] The longer you wait, the harder it becomes to lead them at all. You set your family's rules, and an infraction requires a commensurate consequence, but make sure that infraction is not the result of your poor planning or lack of enabling (the last "E" in the EDGE Method).

Does your child whine? Would you like them to stop? Whining is a learned trait. If you grant your child's desires based on their protestation, you teach them that this is how they get what they want, and you create a whiner. Correct this now. The world does not reward whining. Neither will older Scouts.

I discovered a simple but effective phrase with our young children: "I do not understand you when you use that voice/speak that way," or "I do not understand you when you *tell* me what you want rather than ask," or the like. Then ignore them. If they get louder, it becomes disobedience, which requires a consequence. Start this early, and be consistent.

Help Your Child Disengage without Conflict

Children fixate on screens. Do not set your child up to fail through unregulated screen time and video game play.[21] Create a regular schedule for homework, Scouts, screen time, video game time, and other activities to reduce frustration. Teach your son or daughter how to budget time early in life to reduce angst and increase peace in your home.

Imagine you are settled into a comfortable chair with your favorite beverage. Your new book has you spellbound, or your favorite show has

---

20. James Dobson, *Parenting Is Not for Cowards: Dealing Confidently with the Frustrations of Child-Rearing*, Tyndale House Publishing, 1987, p. 93.

21. Sara Bean, "'Does My Child Have a Video Game Addiction?' How to Set Limits Around Video Game Use," *Empowering Parents.com*, viewed February 23, 2023, www.empoweringparents.com/article/does-my-child-have-a-video-game-addiction-how-to-set-limits-around-video-game-use.

captivated you. Someone interrupts and says, "Time to stop, right now. Go wash your hands and get ready for supper." You would be frustrated or angry. Why do that to your child and undermine their desire to obey you? (Yes, your children want to please you. Help them!)

We used a very effective tool called the five-minute rule.[22] Tell your child they need to wrap up their activity in five minutes. Some people set a timer. A pattern of first-time compliance earns the right to negotiate—within reason. "My show is almost over. May I finish it first?" "We are almost finished with our game. Can we each have two more turns?" Notice the common element in those conversations. The child brings you new information (the show is almost over; the game is nearing the end) and asks permission. They are ready to comply but ask for grace. Say yes when possible, but not every time.

Your Role in the Den and Pack

What is the role of the parents of a new Scout in the pack? You followed the guidance in the last chapter, found a unit aligned with your family's values, joined with other families you know, and your Scout is in a den with their friends, or joined a pack and looks forward to new friends. Great start!

At your first meeting, you join your beaming parent peers watching your little Scouts sport their tiny Cub Scout uniforms. You see through those blue Cub Scout shirts to the tan uniform with a full merit badge sash worn on your future Scout's Eagle court of honor as they launch lifelong friendships.

The Cubmaster asks which of you is the den leader.

Blank stares all around, foreheads shimmering with sweat, hearts beating faster.

---

22. For other helpful transition techniques, visit www.scholastic.com/parents/family-life/social-emotional-learning/technology-and-kids/7-fuss-free-ways-to-turn-tv.html.

Who has the time?

It could be you.

Dens form the core of a pack, with most activity at the den level under adult leadership. No need to panic. You join most parents if you think you are too busy to add this to your task list. The structure of Cub Scouts makes it easy to share or distribute the responsibility if that is the best solution for you and the other parents.

Are you the parent who has dreamed of leading your child's den since their birth, eager to become the Cubmaster? Slow down! Avoid pack-level leadership during the first year to learn how Scouting operates today—it differs from when you were a Scout. Focus on the den's success first.

If you decide to lead or co-lead, does it feel more like you've added to your already over-scheduled life? Or like you are embarking on a new family pastime? Do you begrudgingly scale back other activities, or do you embrace unexpected adventures to find new ways to relate to your child? Attitude makes a difference. "The days are long, but the years are short."[23] You might just find your Scouting life and friendships so fulfilling that they replace those other hobbies permanently. You would not be the first. The gift of involvement in your child's world will outlive you as you become a better parent than your parents (even if they were great), and your children improve on what they learn from you. Change the world, one child at a time—yours!

For those who take on or share den leadership, your local Scout shop and the Internet have myriad helpful resources. Packs often have Lion Cub or Tiger Cub coaches, who are adult leaders who support the parents of new Scouts as they navigate the program and the pack. If your unit does not, model problem-solving, find a mentor in an older Cub Scout's parent. Teach your child. Explain the benefits of asking for help from

---

23. Gretchen Rubin, *The Happiness Project, Tenth Anniversary Edition: Or, Why I Spent a Year Trying to Sing in the Morning, Clean My Closets, Fight Right, Read Aristotle, and Generally Have More Fun*, Harper Paperbacks, 2018.

those more experienced. Demonstrate how to wait for an opportune time, and then how to introduce yourself. Do not waste opportunities to teach.

Pack committee meetings inform you how the pack works and how Cub Scouting works, and they prepare you to support the pack in the future. If you cannot attend, ensure another den parent does.

Does this mean you never miss a pack meeting or den outing? Of course not. Should the single parent feel guilty when they need a break? No! Some seasons of life or family dynamics affect a parent's ability to take part. Find a way that you can support the den while considering your commitments. When you cannot attend an event, dedicate time afterward to talk to your Scout. Ask them to teach you what they learned.

Recommended Adult Training

Begin your swim in the Scouting waters with training. Take YPT, which is required to camp with or lead Cubs. Visit www.scouting.org for details about other courses you should take as you are able, including:

+ **Basic leader training** teaches you what *should happen* in your child's phase of Scouting to guide your Scout and reduce your uncertainty or anxiety.

+ **BALOO training** prepares you to camp with Cub Scouts. Even if your family camps often, you camp with friends, or you are an Eagle Scout who has spent hundreds of nights under the stars, BALOO teaches the methods Scouting America uses today.

+ **Wood Badge**[24] is a much greater time commitment but well worth the investment. You experience Scouting from Lion Cub to Eagle Scout, make new friends, and develop valuable connections. I waited

---

24. www.scouting.org/training/adult/woodbadge.

until my son was in Scouting America to take Wood Badge because I thought it was only for parents with older Scouts, or leaders. I was wrong. Attend as soon as you can.

ADVANCEMENT

Advancement is one Scouting method, but not the only one. Cub Scouts complete at least one-third of the Lion to Bear rank adventures (activities) at home, including almost all of those for the "duty to God" adventures for each rank. Thus, Cub Scouting is largely you and your Scout trying activities together. How well they learn depends on how seriously you take the requirements and how deeply you engage with your Scout. The tasks are fun and open to the whole family, but you are also teaching your Scout how to set and accomplish goals. Even if you do not lead the den, you still lead your child.

Cubs learn indirectly through "games with a purpose" and fun, trying new things with friends. From the Scouting America website, "Cub Scouting is about 'doing'"—i.e., your *Scout* doing, not you doing. If you are more focused on other parents' perception of you or your child than on your child making new friends, growing in confidence, and learning skills, you need the self-awareness to let another parent lead while you kill your pride.

But you are not "that parent." You encourage your Scout and the den to try adventures, and then you stay out of their way. Excellent, within reason. Support the den when they struggle (and let them struggle), comfort them in failure (but let them fail), and rejoice together in success. Know their limits to avoid creating frustration, but still stretch them. EDGE them—Explain, Demonstrate, Guide, and Enable them. Give space for a Scout's ability to surprise you. Help build confidence to benefit your child in Scouts, in school, and in friendships.

Consider the abilities and short attention span of a young child when you plan adventures. Limit sitting-still activities to about one minute per year of age. Cub Scouts need free time to visit or play physical games to get the wiggles out and to prepare them to focus on activities or advancement elements later. Provide healthy but fun snacks so the Scouts have the stamina to finish the activities.

Years ago, one often heard "Fun with a purpose" associated with Cub Scouts. While this phrase is no longer used, the principle is powerful for young Scouts. My generation played outside after school. Today, children often live over-scheduled lives, with hours of homework beginning in early primary or elementary school. For Cub Scouts to "take hold," it must be fun. Baden-Powell said, "A boy is not a sitting-down animal." How true this is for Lion to Bear Cubs!

"Do your best" was the old Cub Scout motto. In Cub Scouts, one measures success by effort, not mastery. As you work through rank elements together, you and your child will discover their natural abilities and affections. Define success through their lens. Help your Scout set challenging but attainable goals, but do not set goals for them. Encourage them to work toward the goals they set without comparison to others.

Successful attempts increase confidence. Failed trials still meet the advancement requirement. Comfort first, then debrief. Was the failure the result of insufficient preparation? Did you have the necessary equipment, and was it in good working order? Did a skill need practice? Does your child lack innate talent in that area? If so, explain how different children have different abilities, without comparison.

Scouting should be a "safe place to fail"—safe from belittling, condemnation, comparison, and/or the dangers created from a lack of preparation. Teach your Scout to do their best, even if that effort fails. Failure is an excellent teacher when you combine it with listening and comforting. Remind your child that your love for them is independent of what they accomplish. Give your Scout the freedom to try new things without fear of disappointing you. Share your failures and what those failures taught you to encourage your child and enhance your relationship. One of my greatest regrets in Scouting and life was not sharing more of my mistakes with my children.

Cub Scouts progress through ranks by age (Lion, Tiger, Wolf, Bear, Webelos, Arrow of Light), and do not have to earn one to move up when the next school year starts. Though not the only Scouting method, advancement is important. During pack meetings or blue and gold banquets, when Scouts receive awards for their accomplishments, if your child is the only one who does not earn something, or the den receives little recognition, they notice. Cub Scout advancement should be frequent and regular to keep Scouts engaged. A lack of advancement discourages Scouts and affects their desire to continue.

Parent sign-off reinforces the family nature of Cub Scouts and helps avoid advancement stalls.[25] However, do not be hasty. Struggle, and the genuine opportunity for failure, make success more rewarding. Cursory approvals do not prepare them for Scouting America, where advancement depends on mastery. Do not ask more than the adventure requires, as this violates Scouting America policies.

Go through optional activities together. Your Scout may have completed requirements during free time or at school, or could, with a little incremental effort. Grow closer as you discover likes and dislikes, and find new areas of interest. One-on-one attention opens the door to your child's world. Look at their handbook during family time and create anticipation for younger brothers and sisters to become Scouts, or older Scout siblings to provide support. Practice as a family, but let your Scout lead. Their increased confidence will overflow into school and other areas of life and help avoid peer pressure.

---

25. "Sign-off" is the process for a Scout to have an approver add their initials for the item in the Scout's handbook.

Advancement at home has to be fun, relationship-building, and stress-free. Cub Scouts burn out under the leadership of an over-zealous parent.

Alternative models: In some countries, and in some units, parents are not involved in Scouting during the meetings. If this describes your program, this section still applies, but more to what you do at home, and increases the need for open-ended questions about meetings to discover your child's strengths and weaknesses. Support the leaders—teach your child joyful obedience at home.

CAMPING

Environment influences learning. A Scout's best classroom is outdoors, away from school, away from comforts, and open to the unexpected. Cub Scouts learn valuable life skills on campouts, yet do not realize they are being taught.

Cub camping is a family event; infrequent but important. The Cub Scout program guide says camping is one of the "ready-made opportunities for your family to do fun things together—because together—we can all grow into our very best future selves!"[26]

If you are in charge of a campout for your child's den (or any meeting or outing), ask your Scout what they consider dull or difficult in the scheduled adventure, and then work together to turn it around. Accept their ideas as often as possible. Prompt them to consider the desires of the other Scouts in the den to help them develop servant leadership, which is where serving others is the top priority. With a little foresight and patience, otherwise mundane activities become opportunities to teach and bond with your child.

Break plans into small pieces so your Scout can take part. Let your Scout help you estimate the costs for an activity to build math skills and

---

26. www.scouting.org/programs/cub-scouts.

"thriftiness" as you evaluate different products at the store and keep a running tab. If you involve Scouts in the planning, you build anticipation and increase the probability of a successful outing.

When you arrive at camp, Scouts need time to burn energy or visit when they arrive, especially if it has been a long drive. Start with free time, then let them know when free time nears its end—the "five-minute warning." Involve the den in the mechanics of camping, not just your child. The Scouts can carry camping gear to the campsite, collect wood for a campfire, or help make dinner. This not only builds teamwork but helps avoid your child "working" while the others play, which helps with obedience.

Your child needs you to let them be a child. When my son and I camped with his pack, we considered the campout a failure if he did not add a stain to his uniform, a scratch to his skin, or a bruise to his body. A child's regulated life offers few opportunities to learn from natural consequences, such as "do not run in woods full of vines at night," "clear your tent site of rocks before going to sleep," or "keep food out of your backpack left outside of the tent" (which becomes a small-animal feeder, or a large-animal snack). We instruct our children. Experience reinforces our instruction.

If Your Scout Wants to Quit

You have done "everything right," but your Scout one day announces that they no longer enjoy Scouting and want to quit. Do other Scouts cause this disquietude? Teach your child problem-solving skills, or how to pursue reconciliation, how to be part of a solution, and ensure they are not part of the problem. Is the issue with parents? Your turn to show them your problem-solving skills and ensure you are not part of the problem.

If your Scout does not enjoy activities because they are not "fun enough," help reshape their perspective. Teach them that fun is only one of a range of activities that satisfy, that completed work provides satisfaction, and the value of delayed gratification.

You and other leaders do your best to make Scouting fun, but some activities may flop. Share your disappointment with the den and brainstorm solutions. Try thorns, roses, and buds as you involve the Cubs to change the activity. Repeat as necessary throughout your child's Scouting career.

COSTS

Uniforms are expensive. A handbook and some camping gear add to the expense. Do not allow the perceived cost of Scouting to dissuade you. If money is a barrier, talk to your pack, district, or council to see if they have used uniforms and other equipment available for free, or at a discount, or whether they offer financial support. When the Scout year begins, some units offer "uniform swaps" or exchanges, or give parents the opportunity to sell equipment and gear they no longer need. In some countries or regions, this is standard practice. If your unit does not have a swap, start one!

FEARS AND CONCERNS

Scouts offers a prime opportunity to help your child overcome their fears of the unknown and fear of failure. Some schools push youth to excel at this age, but in Cub Scouts, your Scout can try new activities without pressure.

If Lion is your child's first rank, Webelos Scouts in the pack are twice their age, and can be twice as big! Help your Scout meet some of those older youth, as friendship will conquer that fear. Those "big Cubs" are not all good role models. Teach your child how to find and befriend those who are. You help when you seek out and befriend their parents. Helpfulness endears young Scouts to those more senior in the pack.

Talk to your child about your fears when you were their age, and how you overcame them. Ignorance breeds fear, so ask questions and teach your Scout how they can find answers when you are not available.

Sample Conversations

Unhelpful

Parent: "Do you like Scouts?"

Scout: "I don't know. Sometimes."

Parent: "You can quit if you want."

Scout: "Maybe."

Parent: "I'll call your den leader."

Helpful

Parent: "Do you like Scouts?"

Scout: "I don't know. Sometimes."

Parent: "What parts do you like?"

Scout: "I like playing with my friends and trying new things. It's fun building forts on campouts. I like our snacks, too."

Parent: "Is there anything you want to try?"

Scout: "I can't wait to be a Webelos Scout. Then I can go camping with the big Scouts and learn to cook and use a knife. On the next campout, can I help you cook?"

Parent: "I would love that. We can practice at home, too. Do you have friends you want to invite to join us in Scouts? It's not too late."

Scout: "A new boy started in my class at school. Can I ask him?"

Parent:	"Of course. Please ask your teacher if it would be okay for me to call his parents to tell them where and when we meet and answer questions they might have."
Scout:	"I'll do that tomorrow."
Parent:	"Thank you for taking that responsibility. Is there anything in Scouts you dislike?"
Scout:	"Sometimes the bigger kids are too rough."
Parent:	"How does that make you feel? Do you have ideas to solve that problem?"
Scout:	"Sometimes it's scary, but I could ask them not to be so rough. If they don't listen, I could ask you to talk to their den leader."
Parent:	"I'm proud of you. You confront your fears and work to solve them. You have good ideas. We can talk about it more before the next meeting, okay?"
Scout:	"Sure. I like going to Scouts."

Unhelpful

Parent:	"You should not try this next activity. You know how uncoordinated you are. You might hurt yourself."
Scout:	"But the other kids are all doing it and they aren't getting hurt."
Parent:	"You get hurt more easily than they do. Let's go home."

Helpful

Scout:	"That game looks hard. I don't know if I can do it."
Parent:	"Just do your best. Remember when you weren't sure you could do an activity and how surprised you were when

you did it? You might learn that there is something you can't do, but you won't know unless you try. You might make a new friend if someone teaches you."

Scout: "That's how I met my best friend in the pack. I'll try it."

Later, on the way home . . .

Parent: "I'm proud of you trying something you weren't sure you could do. How did it go?"

Scout: "It was too hard for me, but the other kids helped me and that made me feel good. I think when I'm bigger I might be able to do it, so I'll keep trying. One day, I want to help the younger kids."

Parent: "I love your attitude!"

RECAP
CUB SCOUTS—LION TO WEBELOS

PARENTING

✤ Enter your child's world.

✤ Set boundaries and rules in an atmosphere of love and acceptance.

✤ Do nothing for your Scout that they can do on their own. Let them struggle a little. Encourage them to recruit their friends or siblings to help.

✤ Be present but do not helicopter.

✤ Learn and practice the EDGE Method at home—prepare your Scout to succeed.

✤ Demonstrate unconditional love, and support your Scout's trials and errors. Do not tie your affection to accomplishments.

✤ Make your home a safe place to fail.

✤ Coach on the field. You and your child "do Scouting" together.

SCOUTING

✤ Ask questions when you first join! Keep asking them when there will be new experiences and challenges.

✤ Observe the unit during the first year, then find your niche to support the pack.

✤ "Try" and "Do Your Best" characterize Cub Scouts.

✤ Ranks are age/grade based, not accomplishment based.

✤ Parents approve most advancement requirements.

✤ Training should look to the Scout like fun activities and games, not replicate school.

✤ Make new friends—both of you.

✤ The whole family can camp together in Cub Scouts.

✤ Adventures reveal tastes and preferences.

✤ Scouting must be a safe place to fail.

✤ Attend pack committee meetings and district or council roundtables.

✤ Get trained!

SIGNS OF SUCCESS

✤ Your Scout looks forward to den and pack meetings.

✤ Your child is excited to share what they have learned.

✤ Your Scout asks when they will get to go camping (or camping again).

✤ They talk to their friends about Scouting.

CHAPTER SEVEN

CUB SCOUTS—ARROW OF LIGHT

*The method of instruction in Scouting is that of creating
in the boy the desire to learn for himself.*

– ROBERT BADEN-POWELL

The good turn will educate the boy out of the groove of selfishness.

– ROBERT BADEN-POWELL

Arrow of Light[27] is an important transition period for both of you. Your Scout needs your support as you walk a fine line between supporting them and letting them go. Lack of preparation during this phase is part of the reason youth drop out of Scouting within a year of their crossover.[28] Your Scout needs to develop basic Scout skills and confidence in using them, and you need to encourage their initiative and independence.

---

27. CUB SCOUTS: Arrow-of-Light; Ages 10–11, 5th Grade; GIRL SCOUTS: Junior; TRAIL LIFE: Navigator; SCOUTS: Cub; GUIDES: Guide; AMERICAN HERITAGE GIRLS: Tenderheart, Explorer

28. "Crossover" is the term used for the transition of Arrow of Light Scouts from Cub Scouts to Scouting America.

The Arrow of Light rank is designed to prepare Cub Scouts to cross-over into Scouting America. Ideally a Cub Scout earns their Arrow of Light award by February and moves into a troop in March of that year. This allows the Scout to become familiar with fellow Scouts and prepare for upcoming summer camps the troop might attend."

These Cub Scouts are the oldest in the pack, and should give back when they help with games and activities. On campouts, your Scout can help unload the car when you arrive, cook, set up and take down your tent, remove trash from the campsite, then help repack when you leave. Involve them in the "work of Scouting," but do not exasperate them. They need time with their friends.

Your child and their den need to help plan more of the activities and events to get them ready for Scouting America, where the Scouts are the planners. Unlike pack events, in troop meetings and campouts, you will be not be as directly involved, so prepare your child. Train them how to lead, with you close, but not hovering. Let them make non-catastrophic mistakes, fail, and try again with your encouragement, careful not to push them to the point of frustration. Debrief with your Scout after meetings. Teach your child how to evaluate why adventures succeeded or failed without criticizing leaders.

Give your son or daughter a lifelong gift: teach them how to make informed decisions. They need a degree of autonomy and empowerment delegated to them. Provide a subset of activities acceptable to you and let them decide. Effective decision-making prepares your Scout for a success-ful crossover and will benefit them in school and other areas of life.

Promote advancement, but make sure you support your Scout's ambitions. You need to encourage, not command. Do not live your goals through them. You can still approve your child's requirements for now, but resist the urge to be their only approver. Teach them how to approach another trusted adult or den chief for sign-off. This will reduce the anxiety when Scout or adult leaders are their exclusive approvers in a troop.

Build Your Relationship

Cub-Scout-aged children need to know that you approve of what they are doing, you are interested in what they are learning, you want to help them, and you are proud of their accomplishments.

Prepare for your child's teen years, where advice and pressure from friends, peers, and other adults may contradict your family's value systems. Children need to feel safest and most supported by their parents as they try to make sense of what they hear and experience. They need love and encouragement from both parents. Establish this now to set your relationship on a trajectory to support and protect them in their middle- and high-school years and beyond. If you do not, someone else will fill that role, and you may not like that someone else, or the guidance they offer.

Move off the field—coach from the sidelines. Teach your Scout at home so they can thrive in meetings and on campouts with less of your involvement. Confidence will make their crossover less intimidating, older Scouts will consider them an asset, and other new Scouts will find a desired teammate. Smooth their transition.

Prepare Your Child for Scouting America

Follow these suggestions to build your Scout's confidence in core Scouting skills to be an asset to their pack and their new troop:

- ♣ **Memorize the Scout Oath, Scout Law, Scout Motto, and Scout Slogan** – Your child will need to learn these for their Arrow of Light and Scout requirements and may be asked to recite them at each board of review for all ranks in Scouting America when you are not there to help them. Though the Scouts recite them *en masse* during troop meetings, memorizing them is important to help a Scout make ethical choices in their life. Practice at home. Print them in large letters and place them somewhere your child will see them often. (Frequent exposure aids in memorization.) Discuss together what each element means. Baden-Powell said, "A boy carries out suggestions more wholeheartedly when he understands their aim." Memorize them with your Scout. Quiz each other in a fun way. Let your child see you struggle.

Memorization help – There are twelve points to the Scout Law. Memorize them in groups of three (trustworthy, loyal, helpful; friendly, courteous, kind . . .). This makes them easier to remember and recall in the correct order.

As you work on the Scout Law together, emphasize the word "is." A Scout's (and Scouter's) life should reflect *every point* in the Scout Law. Each is equally important. They are not simply words to memorize—they are character qualities to live.

+ **Act like a Scout** – Scouts who scream (particularly a high-pitched scream), push, or pester for attention, then run to a parent when an older Scout reacts, find it difficult to be accepted into a troop. Help them transition from young-child behavior to young-adult behavior. Share stories about adjustments you made at their age, including both what you did well and what you wish you had done differently.

+ **Practice servant leadership** – Model servant leadership for your child. Volunteer and look for ways to help, and they will follow your lead. This gift yields lifelong benefits. You and your Scout should both be more involved in pack meetings and outings, helping new Scouts and families in the pack. Helping develops servant leadership.

♣ **Set up, take down, and repack your tent** – Practice! Use the EDGE Method (see the "Scout Parenting Foundations" chapter for details). Work with your Scout to set up the tent they will use on campouts. (If you plan to buy a tent, get advice from parents of older Scouts.) Once you have taught them how to set up, take down, and repack the tent with your help, step aside and have them practice the EDGE Method as they teach a sibling, friend, or other Scout—without your help. The ultimate challenge: to set it up alone—in the dark, in the wind and rain, when it is cold. Arrow of Light Scouts often cross over in winter or early spring. When they set up camp, it will be dark for the first few campouts. It may also be wet and windy. Help them "be prepared!" Repeat these steps whenever they get a new tent, rent, or borrow one—especially if you rent or borrow one! I have seen otherwise confident Scouts (and Scouters) fail with an unfamiliar tent. Morning comes, and the Scout emerges from another Scout's crowded tent, while the adult falls out of their car, nursing a sore back.

♣ **Pack for a campout** – Use the Socratic method (ask questions, rather than give direction) to guide your Scout as they decide what clothing and gear they will need, then show them how to pack it.[29] Unpack and have them repack. Offer guidance only after they have struggled, but not to the point of frustration. Load the car together. At the campground, give the Scouts some run-around or socializing time. After their five-minute warning expires, have them move gear to the campsite together, then assist other fami-

---

29. "The Socratic Method of Teaching: What It Is, Its Benefits, and Examples," St. Leo University Blog, October 12, 2022, www.saintleo.edu/about/stories/blog/socratic-method-teaching-what-it-its-benefits-and-examples.

lies. If your Scout forgets something, unless it is a safety concern (e.g., the weather is cold and wet and they did not bring a coat), resist the urge to rescue them. The probability of forgetting that item next time will drop precipitously if they have to suffer without it. Natural consequences are effective teachers. One of my son's teachers was his patrol's "jerky sandwich" meal. The grub master forgot to buy lunch meat, so all they had was bread, the jerky they had brought for snacks, and mustard. They did not starve, nor did they ever forget lunch meat again. At a later campout, they over-corrected and every Scout in the patrol brought a pound of bacon. They ate it all.

♣ **Cook** – Teach your child how to prepare some basic camp meals. Find hobo pie, omelets in a bag, pancakes, shepherd's pie, and other tasty meal ideas in books available from your local Scout shop, other parents, or the Internet. Make cooking a regular den activity. Snacks do not have to be prepackaged. EDGE the den, so they can prepare a meal without you. If you are the grub master, include them as you plan, shop, and pack. Show them how to keep food cold and avoid contamination. In Scouting America, adults cook and eat separately from Scouts. If you can afford to purchase camp cooking gear, you and your Scout will have more opportunity to practice. There were times our son would cook for us outside, using our camping kit, just for fun. If you do not have what you need, ask to borrow equipment from other pack parents or a troop your Scout may join. Asking can ingratiate your young Scout with older Scouts who see them preparing to move up. You also gain another cook in your house who can help the family and an additional avenue to build your relationship.

♣ **Clean-up** – Opening a cooler or stove or chuck box for the next campout to discover a science experiment initiated on the last outing is an interesting but unpleasant experience. Your child needs to learn the clean-up procedure used by the troop they will join, but one time-tested process you can practice has these five steps (note that none of them includes a dishwasher):

1. Use a paper towel to wipe off remaining food into a trash bag—the dish or utensil should be free of large food particles.

2. Wash dishes, silverware, etc., in warm soapy water—as warm as possible without scalding.

3. Rinse dishes in warm water—as warm as possible without scalding.

4. Rinse in a cool-water tub, with a few drops of bleach added.

5. Hang in a mesh bag, or lay out on paper towels or dish towels to dry.

Learn about Big Scouts

✤ **Visit Scouting America troops** – Troops need new Scouts as older youth age out. New Scouts need a troop. Great match. Attend a few regular meetings—those units familiar or recommended to you. If you do not know where to start, talk to your district leaders or the families who preceded you. Many units maintain an informative website. Ask questions from the list in Appendix C of this book. Involve your Scout in the decision. Talk to your child about what they liked and disliked. Listen closely—you might learn something new about them! Share what you observed as well.

✤ **Camp with Scouting America troops** – Over the summer, or just after school starts, contact troops to determine which of their campouts are open to visitors. Ask early to maximize your options.

Troops plan their campouts to meet the needs of their Scouts, not visitors. Closed outings are a sign of a healthy unit (unless they are all closed!). Camp to see the real troop. Down time provides opportunities to ask about dues, other costs, gear, discounts, and fundraising activities. Expand your Scouting network and make new friends. Your Scout will.

Before you go, talk to troop representatives to set expectations. Do visiting Scouts and parents share a tent (as in Cub Scouts), or camp separately (as in Scouting America)? Prepare your child prior to the campout and debrief together on your way home. What new skills did they learn? What differences did they notice between Scout camping and Cub camping? Did they see any leadership skills they would like to adopt? Can they envision themselves in that troop? Why or why not?

On a campout with much older Scouts, your child may be exposed to topics that unsettle or disturb them (dating, sexual activity, drug use, social media use, cyber-bullying). Develop your active listening skills. Pay close attention to concerns or fears they may not express directly, may not know how to address, or may not even recognize. Your child needs to feel comfortable enough with you to ask you about *any* topic. These conversations will help ease their fears, give you the chance to discuss your family's values, and why you hold them. If you see a difference in your child's behavior, including withdrawal or a shift from openness with you to silence, dive deeper. Do not skip this step, even if it is awkward for you. Be gentle and ask nonjudgmental questions. Comfort them and then help them process what they heard, considering your values. Years of entering their world and developing your relationship are for times like this.

♣ **Participate in council and district events** – Scouting America has many resources to assist your child to cross over to a troop. If your district has a weekend event where Scouting America troops host Webelos and Arrow of Light Scouts, attend it so that your child and their peers can compare several troops in one place. This is an excellent opportunity for you to interview adult leaders while your Scout learns new skills taught by older Scouts. Do not withhold questions. Make sure you find a unit that fits your child's goals and your family's values. Alternate time with the den and adults. "Tent shop" different designs. Ask troop parents about gear and the troop. Debrief as a den and with your Scout. Discover what they learned about the other troops—and themselves.

For more information on transition expectations specific to Arrow of Light Scouts to Scouting America, I recommend chapter four of *The Unofficial Parent Handbook: A Compendium of Practical Information on Scouts BSA for Scout Parents*, under the subheading: "Differences between Cub Scouts and Scouts BSA."[30]

Celebrate Your Arrow of Light Scout

The Arrow of Light badge of rank is a significant accomplishment. Most Cub Scouts who earn it have been in Cub Scouting for three years or longer—a lifetime in child years. Your pack should have a crossover ceremony to transition from Cub Scouts to Scouting America. If they do not, ask other parents, other packs, or search the Internet for ceremonies,

---

30. David Howell, *The Unofficial Parent Handbook: A Compendium of Practical Information on Scouts BSA for Scout Parents*, Howell ATX Publishing, LLC, 2022, p. 80.

arrow wrapping plans, and plaques or other award ideas. Do not miss this opportunity to celebrate your Scout.

Beyond the pack event, consider celebrating your Scout with extended family, or as a den with all families present. Prepare a brief speech to affirm the growth you have seen. Each parent should recognize each Scout, but keep it to a few minutes. You are honoring them, but Arrow of Light Scouts still have short attention spans. Memories of these events last a lifetime. Your child will "remember when" during times of sadness or disappointment. Give your Scout the gift of affirmation.

Recommended Adult Training

Activities you can do to prepare for your transition to a Scouting America parent:

- ♣ **Specific training** – Consider Scoutmaster training to network and learn to better understand Scouting, even if you have no plans to pursue that role. Model preparedness to help your child prepare. There are many online training courses through Scouting America that may interest you, and it is never too early in your Scouter career to take Wood Badge. Plan to retake YPT if yours is expiring.

- ♣ **Attend district or council roundtables** – Network. Visit Scouting America sessions at the roundtable while your child is an Arrow of Light Scout. Get the real scoop on a troop by getting to know its adult leaders. If your prospective troop does not attend district and council meetings and events, ask more questions. Independence from the larger Scouting community is not a good practice in most cases.

Costs

Scout uniforms are durable but expensive. Webelos (fourth grade) can wear a blue uniform, where Arrow of Light Scouts eventually switch to the tan Scouting America uniform. When your Scout changes to a Scouting America uniform is ultimately a family decision. You may choose to wait to buy a Scouting America uniform until after your Scout has earned their Webelos badge of rank since that badge goes on the Scouting America tan uniform shirt. You may choose to wait until after they have completed their fourth grade year and are officially an Arrow of Light Scout. The most practical time would be when your child outgrows their blue shirt, typically during the fourth grade. If cost is a barrier, talk to your pack, district, council, or local Scout shop to find out what financial aid is available or if used clothing and other gear are available at a discount.

Should Mom or Dad Be More Involved?

Increase same-gender Scouting during the Arrow of Light years—moms get more involved with daughters' units and fathers get more involved with sons' units. Same-sex role models increase in importance as children mature, as they learn to become men and women. The other parent should not avoid Scouting, but be less involved in camping and direct training. Both parents should join the pack committee, which is especially important in smaller units with fewer people available to help. Each parent should ensure they camp at least once a year for a front-row seat to watch their child mature.

Fears and Concerns

Your Arrow of Light Scout will be excited to be one of the pack's oldest Scouts, but might be afraid as one of the youngest visitors at a Scouting

America troop meeting or campout, with Scouts as old as seventeen. Not all big Scouts are nice and helpful. Your Scout will be farther away from you at a troop meeting than they are accustomed to in pack meetings, which may undermine their confidence. If they know a Scout in the unit from school or your place of worship, it eases the transition.

Reassure your child that, while you will not be involved in every event, you have confidence in their ability to excel. Debrief with your Scout after meetings and campouts. Give your Scout uninterrupted time to discuss likes, dislikes, and concerns. Ask them about topics they heard discussed but did not understand, Scouting or otherwise.

SAMPLE CONVERSATIONS

Unhelpful

Parent: "Are you ready to join Scouting America next year?"

Scout: "I'm not sure I'm ready. The kids were so big in the last troop the den leader took us to visit, and the meeting was kind of crazy."

Parent: "Sounds like those kids need some discipline. The Scoutmaster needs to learn how to lead them better. I think we should find a different troop."

Scout: "But we all want to join that troop. I have friends from church in that troop."

Parent: "I'll find you a troop that is better organized. Go finish your homework, then go to bed."

Helpful

Parent: "Are you ready to join Scouting America next year?"

Scout:	"I'm not sure I'm ready. I'm still kind of scared of the big kids in the troops we visited, and the meetings were kind of crazy."
Parent:	"Scouting America differs from Cub Scouts. Scouts run the troop, not parents. The Scouts are learning how to lead, like you are. What skills do you have that you could use to help the troop?"
Scout:	"I'm a good listener, and people tell me I have good ideas to help solve problems."
Parent:	"Those are important skills! You will do more with your patrol and learn from older Scouts, not parents. You can teach me what you learn. That will help you remember. Do you think you and your little brother could put up our tent together without my help?"
Scout:	"You taught us that last month, and we've practiced twice after school. One day it was windy and really hard, but we did it."
Parent:	"Wow! I'm so proud of you. You will be ready for Scouting America. Could we try it in the dark, one weekend? You could spend the night in the backyard. Would you like that?"
Scout:	"Could we really? I'll take the battery-powered lantern in case Brian gets scared. I'll tell him happy stories before we go to sleep."
Parent:	"You will be a big help to your new troop."

PARENT–DAUGHTER CONVERSATION

Unhelpful

Parent: "How was the campout?"

Daughter: "It was okay. I don't want to talk about it."

Parent: "Why not? Wasn't it fun?"

Daughter: "Sometimes it was weird."

Parent: "You'll get used to it. You just need to grow up."

Helpful

Parent: "How was the campout?"

Daughter: "It was okay. I don't want to talk about it."

Parent: "You can talk to me about anything. I love you. Sometimes older Scouts discuss topics you have not experienced, and that can be scary. Some families allow things we do not. That can be confusing."

Daughter: "Yeah. One of the older girls talked about things she does with her boyfriend. To think that boys do those things to girls scared me."

Parent: "I can see how uncomfortable that made you. Not every boy is a thoughtful gentleman. It is best not to be alone with another boy, except your brother, just as you should not be alone with another adult other than one of us. If you end up alone with someone and you should not be, call us, or send an SOS on your phone, and we will come get you. When it is time for you to have a boyfriend, we will talk to you about the rules we have established to protect you."

Daughter: "Thank you. I'm thankful you will protect me. I think next time I'll hang out with some other girls because those discussions make me uncomfortable."

Parent: "You are expanding your problem-solving skills. We love you. Our job is to protect you. If your friends want to do something that you do not, blame us. You could say, 'My parents won't let me do that, or go there, or talk like that, or see that movie, or read that book,' or whatever. Just tell us afterward, in case your friend asks us, so we can support what you said."

Daughter: "I love you."

PARENT–SON CONVERSATION

Unhelpful

Parent: "How was the campout?"

Son: "It was okay. I don't want to talk about it."

Parent: "Why not? Wasn't it fun?"

Son: "Sometimes it was weird."

Parent: "You'll get used to it. You just need to grow up."

Helpful

Parent: "How was the campout?"

Son: "It was okay. I don't want to talk about it."

Parent: "You can talk to me about anything. I love you. Sometimes older Scouts discuss topics you have not experienced, and that can be scary. Some families allow things we do not. That can be confusing."

Son:	"Yeah. One of the older guys talked about things he tries to do with girls. It sounded kind of gross and also mean."
Parent:	"I can see how uncomfortable that made you. We have tried to raise you to be a thoughtful gentleman, but not all boys are raised that way. On our walk this weekend, let's talk more about how to treat girls respectfully. You can ask me about anything you heard and I will answer you honestly."
Son:	"You always do. Thank you. I'm thankful you want to help me. I think next time I'll hang out with some other guys because I don't like talking that way."
Parent:	"You are expanding your problem-solving skills. We love you. Our job is to protect you. If your friends want to do something that you do not, blame us. You could say, 'My parents won't let me do that, or go there, or talk like that, or see that movie, or read that book,' or whatever. Just tell us afterward, in case your friend asks us, so we can support what you said."
Son:	"I love you."

RECAP

CUB SCOUTS—ARROW OF LIGHT

- Enter your son or daughter's world. Comfort and encourage them as it changes.

- Invest in your relationship for immediate returns and to prepare for the teen years.

- Reinforce your family's values as you navigate topics you both wish your Scout had not heard from older Scouts (or friends, fellow students, or older siblings).

- Teach your child how to make informed decisions commensurate with their age.

- Affirm your child's growth in skills and leadership.

- Debrief with your Scout after meetings and outings you cannot attend and those you do.

- Increase the ratio of questions to directions as you train your Scout to lead.

- Help your Scout develop their problem-solving skills.

- Be your child's trusted advisor.

♣ Keep home a safe place to fail.

♣ Coach from the sidelines. Move off the field.

SCOUTING

♣ The Arrow of Light rank provides the link between Cub Scouts and Scouting America, and develops the skills necessary to continue the Scouting journey.

♣ Advancement requirements grow in complexity and required effort to help prepare your Cub Scout for Scouting America.

♣ Webelos and Arrow of Light dens have increased interaction with Scouting America units, but are still part of the pack.

♣ Your Scout will become more independent on campouts.

♣ Your older Cub Scout should be more involved in planning to prepare them for Scouting without you.

♣ You should each lead in the den and pack, and help younger Scouts and their parents.

♣ Scouting must be a safe place to fail.

♣ Attend pack committee meetings and district or council roundtables.

♣ Get trained!

Signs of Success

- Your Scout can set up and repack their tent and camping gear by themselves or with help from peers.

- Younger Scouts ask them for help.

- Peers seek their help and look to them as a leader.

- From the prior *Webelos Handbook*: "Your child sees Webelos Scouting as a chance to have fun, go camping, and make new friends. They also see it as a step on the way to outdoor adventures in Scouting."

- Your Scout is confident in asking other adult leaders to sign for advancement.

- Your child's Arrow of Light den is comfortable interacting with the youth in a Scouting America troop and has decided on the one they want to join.

CHAPTER EIGHT

SCOUTING AMERICA— SCOUT TO FIRST CLASS

When Scouting has failed it has been because we have departed from the Patrol System and have failed to trust the boys with responsibility, because we have made our Scouting too nearly a school subject and not a life of joyous adventure.

— THOMAS CORBETT, CHIEF SCOUT,
HANDBOOK FOR BOYS, 1951

There is no teaching to compare with example.

— ROBERT BADEN-POWELL

You and your Scout have found a troop that aligns with your family's values after asking the right questions from Appendix C.[31] Your once-

---

31. SCOUTING AMERICA: Scout to First Class; Ages ~10–14 years; GIRL SCOUTS: Cadet, Senior; TRAIL LIFE: Navigator, Adventurer; SCOUTS: Scout, Explorer; GUIDES: Guide, Ranger; AMERICAN HERITAGE GIRLS: Explorer, Pioneer.

excited and confident Arrow of Light Scout may now be anxious and insecure. Youth as old as seventeen, giants compared even to you, unintentionally intimidate new Scouts because of their physical maturity and Scouting ability. Some do so intentionally.

If your child is new to Scouts, discuss school or other transitions to reassure them. Share success and failure stories from your life changes.

If your Scout spent several years in Cub Scouts, remind them when they were the youngest and smallest, and how they grew and became a leader. This will build their confidence.

Did you practice the activities in the "Prepare Your Child for Scouting America" section from the last chapter to ready yourselves to move up? If not, do so! If you did, you should be ready for Scouts—for your child to learn new skills from the giant Scouts, and you to let them. Scouting America is no place for a helicopter parent.

The basic operational component of Scouts is the patrol, which should contain six to eight Scouts. This is the group with whom your child will spend most of their time. Baden-Powell placed a high value on this structure: "The patrol system is not one method in which Scouting can be carried on. It is the only method." Talk to troop leaders to learn how they assign new Scouts to patrols. For Scouts who cross over from Cub Scouts together, it can work well for them to form a patrol with a troop guide to teach them how to navigate the troop and Scouting program. If you were a Scout, the philosophy for the ideal patrol composition has changed. YPT standards dictate that Scouts in a patrol cannot differ in more than two years of age, and Scouting America encourages the use of age-based patrols.[32]

Step back and become a student again. Scout-led troops are messy. My son's first meeting baffled me, accustomed to a Fortune 100 business setting. My misunderstanding, misguided brain told me that was no way

---

32. scouting.org/health-and-safety/gss.

to run a meeting! In wisdom that surprises me looking back, I waited and watched the program unfold, slower than my efficiency-oriented brain would like, but work it did. Rambunctious boys grew into responsible young men of character.

When your Scout joins a troop, they also join a new social unit. If they earned their Arrow of Light rank, they finished as one of the oldest and biggest. Now they are among the youngest and smallest. This key transition at this age prepares your child for successful future life changes (high school, college, work, place of worship, etc.). Practice shaking hands with a firm (not bone-crushing) grip and eye contact so that they create a confident first impression with Scouts and adults.

Observe and discuss how older Scouts respond to new Scouts and to youth and adult Scout leaders. Teach your child how to identify positive role models and introduce themselves. Help them see the "big" Scouts who model Scouting ideals as versions of their future selves.

Encourage your Scout to find and associate with outstanding leaders on their path to become one. Discuss the positive attributes these leaders demonstrate. If troop leadership is weak, ask your child what they would do differently, but do not defame anyone's character. If there is a potential safety concern, teach your Scout to follow the chain of command in the troop (patrol leader, then assistant senior patrol leader, then SPL, then Scoutmaster). Serious safety concerns, however, require an immediate conversation with the SPL and Scoutmaster.

If the standard of behavior in the troop overall worries you, talk to the parents of older Scouts. All may not be as it appears. Heed Baden-Powell's advice: "If you make listening and observation your occupation, you will gain much more than you can by talking." If you are not satisfied, discuss your concerns with the committee chair, or schedule time with the Scoutmaster. (Unless there is an immediate safety concern, do not distract the Scoutmaster during the meeting.) If your Scout is part of the problem, teach them to own their actions, apologize, and reconcile, then affirm them when they do.

Not all Scouts live the Scout Oath and Scout Law. There may be a "wrong crowd" in the troop or camp. Our daughter worked at a Scouting America summer camp and expected all the young men to behave like her younger brother and his patrol, who respected authority, behaved like gentlemen, were maturing in their faiths, and exhibited leadership skills with a desire to serve. Several fellow counselors, to her dismay, were not model Scouts. Some did not even come close. Poor behavior in others is a teaching moment for your child. (Our daughter worked with camp and council leaders to make improvements.) Together, set standards of conduct aligned with Scouting ideals and your religious convictions.

ADVANCEMENT: FIRST CLASS FIRST

You want your child to succeed. Your Scout's Eagle is out there, but they need prodding, right? They will not finish unless you push, right?

Do yourself and your Scout a favor: do not rush and do not push. Scouting is a process, not a race. If they rush to reach First Class, a Scout will not develop expertise. Troops often encourage new Scouts to complete their First Class rank within a year or soon after their first summer camp: slowly enough to develop the foundational skills on which the rest of Scouting builds, yet moving through advancement elements to create a sense of accomplishment. Unlike Cub Scouts, where a Scout only has to try in order to advance, in Scouting America they must show mastery on their own or with Scout peers. You can help at home, but your Scout has to demonstrate their abilities to an instructor, assistant Scoutmaster, or the Scoutmaster without you.

In this short period, your child will learn more core skills than in any other phase of Scouting. In a well-functioning, Scout-led troop, you might perceive chaos during which, somehow, older Scouts teach your child valuable life lessons and outdoor acumen. A Scout who works toward First Class develops competence in first aid, camping, and leadership, improves their physical fitness, learns about their environment, and works effectively in a team, even if they do not complete the rank. Your Scout will be prepared for the unexpected on school outings and be a hero with their knot-tying talent or first-aid expertise.

Encourage your Scout to teach you, a sibling, or a friend what they learn using the EDGE Method. Give them opportunities to hone their skills with you outside of Scout events. Remind them to start with their *Scout Handbook* when they need help, to reflect Baden-Powell's suggestion: "In Scouting, a boy is encouraged to educate himself instead of being instructed." With others (at the family dinner table, for example), ask your Scout to demonstrate what you know they have mastered. These esteem boosts build self-confidence that flows into other areas of life as well.

Your Scout should not rush through requirements, but you do not want them to stall either. Scouts who fall behind their peer group often become discouraged, and some do not recover. The *Scout Handbook* breaks advancement into achievable steps. "How does one go about eating an elephant? . . . You eat it one bite at a time."[33] The Scoutmaster and other adults should help them set reasonable goals during Scoutmaster conferences and boards of review. Study and practice together. Show genuine interest in their Scouting activities, encourage them to stretch themselves, but let your Scout's goals be their own.

First Class is a significant accomplishment. Support your child. If they stall along the way, encourage them and help them recognize the opportunities that this first major milestone on their path to Eagle presents. Order of the Arrow, National Youth Leadership Training (NYLT), National Advanced Youth Leadership Experience (NAYLE), high-adven-

---

33. Desmond Tutu, quoted from the 2011 film *I Am*, directed by Tom Shadyac.

ture programs (Philmont, Northern Tier, Sea Base, and Summit Bechtel) are limited to those Scouts who have earned their First Class rank or higher. Some troops also restrict some leadership positions to those who have earned advanced ranks.

Advancement develops initiative. A Scout must determine when they are prepared, then follow their troop's sign-off process to find a qualified leader, then demonstrate mastery. Some troops prefer approvals before and after regular troop meetings. Others sign off at campouts or during dedicated advancement meetings. Some do not have a fixed time.

Though you practice together at home, stay out of sight when your Scout pursues sign-offs. You add to your Scout's stress and increase their nervousness if you hover, or remain in sight. They do not want to disappoint you. Do not bribe or threaten, which deprives your son or daughter of the sense of satisfaction gained by reaching a goal they set for themselves.

If your Scout follows the troop's process to the letter, they could still be told "no." Their target approver could be busy or unqualified, the correct gear might not be available, or your child may not have mastered the requirement. Teach them to follow through—is there someone else who can help? Does your child need more practice or study? "No" in advancement is actually "wait" or "try again."

When your Scout fails to master a requirement, especially after a few tries, encourage them with Thomas Edison's view of failure: "I have not failed 10,000 times—I have successfully found 10,000 ways that will not work."[34] Provide a safe place to fail. Help them learn from their unsuccessful attempts. Support them with examples from your life, what your setbacks taught you. What a gift to give a child: Teach them to use failure to discover innate abilities, skills they can develop, and some tasks they

---

34. Erica Hendry, "7 Epic Fails Brought to You by the Genius Mind of Thomas Edison," *Smithsonian Magazine*, November 20, 2013, www.smithsonianmag.com/innovation/7-epic-fails-brought-to-you-by-the-genius-mind-of-thomas-edison-180947786.

may never master. I could practice piano every day and improve but never compete in world competitions. Help your Scout challenge themselves, yet set realistic goals.

Study your child. Help them determine their natural talents and abilities. Combine these with their likes and dislikes to guide them into the best version of themselves. In Scouting, youth try a diverse range of activities, stretch themselves to test their limits, find new likes and dislikes, and refine their identity. You may find Scouting does the same for you.

Invest in Your Child . . .
Before It Is Too Late

You have only two to four more years as your child's primary influencer if they join Scouts as a ten- to twelve-year-old. You have no time to waste! Take advantage of teaching moments.

The drive or walk home from Scout meetings, to and from school, or to and from campouts provide ready-made opportunities to enter your child's world and learn about their Scouting experiences, which often opens a door to discussions about other areas of life. This intentional time with your child will deepen your relationship.

Ask open-ended questions: "What were your thorns and roses? Any buds?" (Your troop may use different names, like lemons and lemonade, or honey and onions—what succeeded or failed, or any new ideas.) "What worked well in the meeting/on the campout? Would you have done anything differently? If so, what, and why?" "How did you help your patrol?" "How do you want to prepare for the next meeting?" "Do you need my help at home?"

Do not stop on the surface. Ask deeper questions. "Did you hear or see anything that made you feel uncomfortable? Are there topics you heard from older Scouts that you want me to explain?"[35] Probe here, especially if your son or daughter becomes uncharacteristically quiet or dismissive. Share from your youth. For example: "When I was your age, older kids used words that we did not use in our home. Just because these kids are older does not make them right." If you have been building an open and honest relationship with your child, they should be ready to share. They do not need to give you names unless there is a safety concern. Do not overreact. (Which can be easier said than done!)

Reinforce your child's capacity to make wise decisions, either based on good decisions they see around them or in response to poor ones. Teach them how to take part in activities and not violate your family's values, and how to remove themselves graciously when needed. Share examples of how you did this—or wish you had. Your vulnerability will encourage them and deepen your relationship.

If you drive home from a campout and your Scout falls asleep, let them rest. Scouts are often exhausted after a full weekend outdoors. Make time for that intentional conversation the next day, over dinner at their favorite restaurant, a visit to your go-to dessert place, or at home—wherever your Scout is most comfortable and most apt to speak freely.

Scouts are works in progress, becoming adults. You are not your child's only character educator. Peers, older Scouts, and other adults also mold them, and their values may or may not align with your value systems or religious convictions. Open dialogue, free of condemnation, will encourage your child to ask you any question and share their observations and concerns. Not the case for your conversations? Change now, before it is too late! You must earn your child's trust—you cannot mandate it. Cherish it and adapt as your child ages to maintain it.

35. Taylor Tropea, "What Teens Think About Peer Pressure—And How Parents Can Help," *Center for Parent & Teen Communication*, October 27, 2022, parentandteen.com/what-teens-think-peer-pressure.

This is a great age to become your child's scapegoat. If you have been working on your relationship, your child should trust you and want to please you. Peers' opinions increase in your child's estimation, so give them an out if they need one. "My parents will kill me if I do that," or "I would be grounded until I graduate if I did that," or similar phrases that allow them to save face and honor their desire to obey you. Warning: Ensure you know what they put on you so you can support them if that friend later asks why you would not permit something. I learned that lesson firsthand.

Scouting Success Strategies

- ✤ **Commit** – You and your Scout should both commit to one year. If you join a troop that just does not fit, change troops—do not quit. The first year involves many challenges and changes, and requires commitment. Model and teach the steadfastness your child needs. Woody Allen once said, "80% of success is showing up."[36]

- ✤ **Dress for success** – What does your Scout's troop consider a Class A uniform, field uniform, dress uniform, or, simply the uniform (versus a Class B uniform or activity uniform)? When does a Scout wear which? Your child will feel more comfortable when they look like the other Scouts. Uniforms can be expensive. If finances are a barrier, talk to the troop, district, or council. Scholarships or other resources could be available, or your Scout could earn the money needed.

- ✤ **Learn troop policies** – When you understand how the troop operates, you help your child and support the troop. Does the troop

---

36. Woody Allen was asked about this saying by William Safire, the language columnist for *The New York Times*, in 1989, and replied, in a letter, "I did say that 80 percent of success is showing up." *The Quote Investigator*, accessed March 4, 2023, quoteinvestigator.com/2013/06/10/showing-up.

have an operations handbook? Do they offer new-parent orientation? If not, ask the troop committee to provide a panel of experienced parents for questions and answers. Share what you learn with your child to help set your expectations. If you were a Scout, ask *more* questions. What you did may not be part of today's program. Some of your favorite memories are almost certainly now forbidden!

♣ **Ask questions** – Model how to ask questions so your Scout can do so without alienating older Scouts. Teach your child to read body language.

♣ **Camp** – Camping teaches your child the essence of Scouting, tests the troop leadership philosophy, and develops outdoor skills. Your child's troop should camp most months. Encourage your Scout to attend them all. The worse the weather, the greater the character building—and the memories. Help out on campouts when needed to support your Scout and their unit, but also give your child space to grow in your absence. Establish a pattern and share your rationale: maybe you commit to every other campout, even if they are the ones with the nasty weather. When you do not go, debrief with your Scout afterward. If your spouse is the designated Scouting parent, then camp once a year. Your Scout will amaze you.

♣ **Send your Scout to summer camp** – Scout summer camp is difficult and uncomfortable, and, in many areas, hot and/or humid. But there are few better chances for your Scout to grow, bond with fellow Scouts, share challenges, make memories, and accomplish tasks without Mom or Dad's help. Scout summer camp is an incredible classroom. Those who abstain tend not to remain in Scouting. Summer camp Scout-to-First-Class programs (called something like Eagle Quest or First Class Trail) provide an amazing repertoire of outdoor and life skills. Build up summer camp as it approaches. Help your Scout develop their problem-solving skills at home. Cut the apron strings: resist the urge to attend their first summer camp if their troop has enough leaders without you. The child you pick up will be dirtier and smell worse than the one you dropped off—but will also be more accomplished, confident, and mature.

♣ **Sign up for troop service projects** – Volunteering helps endear younger Scouts to their older peers, introduces you both to other Scouts and Scouters, and can meet the service hour requirements necessary for rank advancement. An added benefit: when you both volunteer for Eagle projects, your Scout will find a ready and willing workforce when it is time for his or her own.

Recommended Adult Training

♣ **Attend troop committee meetings** – What are the troop's plans? What do they need? How you can help? The troop committee has these answers. Your child's troop should encourage all parents to attend. Closed meetings or discouraging attendance are cause for concern.

♣ **Specific training** – Take YPT if yours is expiring. While you have time during your "gap year," complete Scoutmaster/Assistant Scoutmaster Training, Troop Committee Training, Weather Hazards Training, or any other training that either interests you or the troop needs someone to have. (If possible, attend your council's Wood Badge course.[37] If you have completed your ticket, the goals you set to improve your unit, apply to staff a course.)

---

37. www.scouting.org/training/adult/woodbadge.

Family Meetings

You leave the house, excited to see your child in action at their first troop meeting. After an awe-inspiring opening, you attend the troop committee meeting and leave overwhelmed by the long list of troop needs.

A few months in and you have answered the call for help—repeatedly. Your excitement is gone, replaced with anxiety over how you will fit your child's new passion into your busy life.

The troop meeting is in thirty minutes and your Scout casually remarks, "I just remembered, I'm teaching how to cook Bananas Foster tonight. Do you have a recipe? Can we stop to get ingredients for fifty people? And I think the stoves need fuel."

Let me introduce you to the family meeting. Find thirty minutes before the start of the week. We did Sunday nights right after dinner.

Each person shares what they have scheduled the coming week beyond the normal routine (school, work, religious services, other recurring activities), plus events or commitments further out in the year. Discuss how to support each person's schedule. Do both parents have extra busy weeks? Could your Scout help one night with those camp cooking skills they have developed?

Teach your child how to plan and you give them a lifelong gift. In college, our son lived with eight other guys in a house. Several had been in Scouts, so they used a modified campout duty roster to ensure a fair distribution of labor and avoid misunderstandings. Consider creating one for your home.

Costs

If you are new to Scouting, warning: uniforms are expensive. (Repeated from the "Cub Scouts–Lion to Webelos" chapter.) A handbook and some camping gear add to the expense. Do not allow the perceived cost of

Scouting to dissuade you. If money is a barrier, talk to your pack, district, or council to see if they have used uniforms and other equipment available for free, or at a discount, or if they offer financial support. At the start of the Scouting year, some units offer uniform swaps or exchanges, or give parents the opportunity to sell equipment and gear they no longer need. In some countries or regions, this is standard practice. If your unit does not have a swap, start one!

Should Mom or Dad Be More Involved?

Practice as much same-gender Scouting as possible—moms help with daughters' troops and fathers help with sons' troops, both the week-to-week activities and campouts.

Dad, be your son's first choice for his "How to be a man" teacher. Mom, be your daughter's first choice for her "How to be a woman" teacher. And each of you strive to be the close second for the opposite-sex child.

Same-sex role models increase in importance as your child grows older, for them and the other Scouts. The troop committee needs you both, especially in smaller troops with limited volunteer pools, and each parent should try to camp at least once a year to get a front-row seat to watch their child mature. Both parents might be merit badge counselors, so one parent is not involved exclusively, but the same-sex parent is more actively engaged.

Fears and Concerns

Youth are eager for responsibility, for the right to make decisions—until they have to make them. Your Scout may be worried about the social or physical consequences of making a poor decision. Practice what-if scenarios. Encourage them to work through a scenario until they get stuck, then guide them as they refine their thought process. Ask questions to help your child discover the answer for him or herself. Wait to share advice until they exhaust their thoughts or cannot decide on an appropriate response.

Some Scouts fear their first summer camp. Talk through their fears, acknowledge them, and help them work to overcome them. There may be spiders and snakes. Some may be venomous. But some Scouts can be more toxic. If your Scout has become an asset to older Scouts through initiative, volunteering, and skills growth, they will more likely find a protector. Share related experiences from your youth and how you overcame your fears.

Scouting offers an additional opportunity to extend and deepen your relationship. A child may open up during your debrief together after a campout, or share worries about developing sufficient skills for a rank advancement. The right questions and active listing can reveal concerns in other areas of life. Listen well. Married parents should also offer each of their children focused time together.

BULLYING

When the ideals of Scouting manifest in a troop, older Scouts mentor younger Scouts, encourage them, and challenge them to do their best. Bullying is the antithesis of Scout ideals. It can lead to abuse, and the consequences can be devastating. If a Scout bullies your child, especially an older Scout, your child needs to report the incident to you, their patrol leader, senior patrol leader, and the Scoutmaster.

Help bully-proof your child. In my experience, the most frequent targets whine and pester the older Scouts, have a limited skill set, and focus on what they want, rather than how they can help. Those who develop their skills, interact with Scouts outside of their patrol, and offer aid are more likely to find support from older Scouts, who will not allow them to become a bully's victim.

Sample Conversations

Unhelpful

Family scattered around the living room, on their phones or watching TV while eating dinner.

Parent:	"Scouts is tonight. I don't know about you, but I'm pretty tired and have a busy day tomorrow. I think we should skip this meeting."
Scout:	"I miss my friends, and I like learning new things."
Parent:	"You can see your friends at the next meeting. And I don't think you would like the things they are doing tonight."
Scout:	"Okay. Can we go to the next one?"
Parent:	"Maybe."

Helpful

Family sitting at the table, eating dinner, no phones, no TV.

Parent:	"Scouts is tonight. Work is busy right now, but helping you learn Scout skills and leadership are important to me. I also enjoy getting to know your friends and their parents."
Scout:	"I have a lot of homework tonight. I'm not sure I have time."
Parent:	"Is there anything I can do to help you?"
Scout:	"Can we get there right when it starts and leave right when it finishes? Sometimes I have to wait for you while you talk to the parents."

Parent:	"Sorry about that. I get carried away sometimes. I'll try to pay attention to the time. If I forget, just come put your hand on my shoulder. That will be our 'time-to-go' sign."
Scout:	"I like that sign. You can do the same with me if I get busy with my friends. Can we also get a milkshake on the way home to help me stay awake while I finish my homework?"
Parent:	"Sure. As long as you eat your vegetables." *Both smile.*

Unhelpful

Parent:	"I think your SPL is incompetent. The Scoutmaster needs to teach them better or find another one."
Scout:	"Our SPL is always friendly to me."
Parent:	"Their job is not to be your friend but to run the troop. Tonight's meeting was chaos. Who can learn in that environment?"
Scout:	"I learned a new game."
Parent:	"You aren't there to learn games. You're there to get your Eagle Scout, so you can get into college."

Scout says nothing and slinks away, dejected.

Helpful

Parent:	"The troop meeting seemed chaotic tonight. Was your SPL having a hard time?"
Scout:	"I don't know. Our SPL is always nice to me and helped me understand the rules of the game we played. The instructor is only two years older than I am. I think I'd like to be an instructor."

Parent: "You would be a great instructor. When we get home, why don't you teach your little sister how to play that game? Did you know that the man who started Scouting, Lord Baden-Powell from England, said over a hundred years ago, 'O God, help me to win, but in your wisdom if I do not to win, then O God, make me a good loser.' I hope you enjoy everything you learn in Scouts. I see you do your best. Whether you win or lose a game, or master or fail what you try, I am proud of you."

Scout: "Thanks. I'm excited to teach you all what I learned. I like trying new things in Scouts."

Unhelpful

Parent: "I saw some of the other boys getting their rank advancements signed off tonight. You're going to fall behind. You should be the one leading the other boys in your patrol. Get your act together."

Scout: "Okay."

Hangs their head, slouches toward their room, and throws their Scout Handbook in the corner with the rest of their uniform; cries in private.

Helpful

Parent: "How are you doing with your advancement? Are you on track to reach your goals?"

Scout: "Sometimes I forget to get my book signed. Our patrol does most things together and we help each other. We work really well together."

Parent: "Teamwork is important in Scouts and outside of Scouts. Do you need anything from me to help you stay up with your sign-offs?"

Scout: "My friend lost their book once, and it was really hard to go back and get sign-offs, so now his dad takes a picture of his handbook sign-off pages every time he gets something signed off. The advancement chair said that's a good idea in case something happens to our books. Would you do that for me?"

Parent: "I would be happy to do that for you. I'll put a reminder on my calendar. You could write a note and put it up in your room. That way, one of us might remember."

Both smile.

Scout: "Can we go early next time? Some of the other Scouts in my patrol also want to go early so that we can compare our handbooks. The advancement chair told us they get to Scouts thirty minutes early for most meetings so that we don't have to miss activities. We might need to go early a few times. Is that okay?"

Parent: "You are growing in your problem-solving skills! That sounds like a splendid solution! We will make sure you get there early whenever you need to. Remind us at our family meeting this week to make sure, but I'll put it on my schedule. I am proud of you."

Scout: "Thanks. I love you."

⚜ ⚜ ⚜

Unhelpful

Parent: "Summer camp registration is tomorrow night. Do you know what merit badges you want to earn? You should get as many as you can."

Scout: "I don't want to go to summer camp. There are bugs, it's hot, and the big kids are mean."

Parent: "Well, you don't have to go if you don't want to."

Scout: "Good. I don't want to."

Parent: "I'll make sure the Scoutmaster doesn't coerce you into going."

Helpful

Parent: "Summer camp registration is tomorrow night. Do you know what merit badges you want to earn?"

Scout: "I don't want to go to summer camp. There are bugs, it's hot, and the big kids are mean."

Parent: "That does not sound like our other summer vacations. What worries you about those things?"

Scout: "If a snake or a spider bites me, I'll die."

Parent: "Has that ever happened at your summer camp?"

Scout: "Well, last year one kid got bitten by a rattlesnake and a black widow spider bit another one."

Parent: "And what happened?"

Scout: "They went to the hospital and got ice cream and air-conditioning and a comfortable bed. We got to ride in the camp bus to go see them, and we got hamburgers on the way home. Those kids became famous in our troop. I guess it wasn't so bad. The leaders at the camp taught us how to avoid being bitten. I think the kid that the snake bit had been teasing it with a stick. The mean kids are scarier than the snakes and spiders."

Parent: "How?"

Scout: "I heard they tied a kid up last year with duct tape."

Parent: "And ... ?"

Scout: "Well, they got in trouble and had to leave camp, and all the other kids helped the littler Scout, so it wasn't too bad. Plus, I'm friends with some of the older Scouts, and I don't think they would let anyone do that to me, and I bet I could help protect my friends as well."

Parent: "Sounds like you are prepared to have a great time at camp."

Scout: "Yeah, I think I am. After talking to you, I'm not as afraid. Thank you."

Unhelpful

Parent: "How many merit badges are you going to earn? I earned sixty when I was a Scout. You should try to get them all."

Scout: "I don't know. I'm just trying to earn First Class with the rest of the guys, and it's hard."

Parent: "You need to practice more and work harder. There is a Merit Badge University coming up, where Scouts can earn merit badges, and then there's the STEM weekend, where you can work on the science and technology merit badges, plus a conservation weekend where you can work on outdoors merit badges. I'll sign you up. And don't forget to finish your homework."

Scout: "Okay."

Grimaces as they stomp to their room.

Helpful

Parent: "Do you have a goal for how many merit badges you want to earn?"

Scout: "I haven't thought about it much. One kid in the troop last year earned them all, and another kid earned about half of them. Earning all of them sounds like a lot, but I think I might want to earn half of them. I'm not sure yet. I know I want to earn at least twenty-one because I want to be an Eagle Scout."

Parent: "Sounds like you are evaluating how to set a healthy, sustainable pace for your advancement. You are wise for not trying to rush. I think it's normal for Scouts to start working on merit badges at summer camp. The troop leaders will help you figure out the best ones to work on when the time is right. Once you decide on your goal, let me know how you want me to help."

Scout: "Thanks. I love the stuff we're learning in our Scout-to-First-Class program."

Parent: "Is there anything you've learned that you could teach the rest of the family? I overheard some of the other Scouts talking to each other about how great you were with knots and lashings, and that if something happened to them, they would want you to perform the first aid."

Scout (*beaming*): "I'll go get some rope and my first aid kit. When can I show everyone? I don't want dinner to get cold."

Parent: "Of course. Thank you for your consideration for the family."

RECAP

SCOUTING AMERICA—SCOUT TO FIRST CLASS

PARENTING

🔱 Spend time in your child's changing world.

🔱 Develop your relationship with your child to prepare you both for the teen years.

🔱 Hold weekly family meetings.

🔱 Ask questions and listen well—your Scout will hear things from older Scouts that you might both wish they had not.

🔱 Listen more than you speak. Master the Socratic method—answer your Scout by asking questions.

🔱 Be a learner. You have a front-row seat to watch the world's best youth leadership training at work.

🔱 Your home must be a safe place to fail.

🔱 Coach more remotely.

SCOUTING

✤ Scouts is a leadership incubator—a messy one. You and your Scout are now part of that mess.

✤ Focus on the core Scout skills needed for First Class and the first summer camp.

✤ Most training should be Scout-to-Scout.

✤ Scouts earn few merit badges during this phase.

✤ The troop should camp every month.

  + Your Scout should take part in all of them.

  + You should participate in some of them (maybe half).

  + Your spouse should go once a year.

  + Your children who are not in the troop should not attend any.

✤ If you find your Scout burning out, read the section "Burnout and Competing Interests" in the next chapter.

✤ Watch and learn as other Scouts and adult leaders teach your Scout.

✤ Debrief with your Scout after troop meetings and campouts.

✤ Attend troop committee meetings and district or council roundtables.

✤ Learn how the troop operates to help your Scout navigate.

✤ Get trained!

Signs of Success

- ✤ Your Scout looks forward to meetings and campouts.

- ✤ Other Scouts approach your child at meetings for help and/or friendship.

- ✤ Your Scout engages in activities during troop meetings and campouts. They might return the worse for wear.

- ✤ Your Scout fails sometimes. (It should mean that they are stretching themselves; make sure you are not pushing them.)

- ✤ Your child confidently pursues youth or adult leaders for help with advancement, and they know when to ask.

- ✤ Your family learns new skills, ones that your Scout is excited to teach you.

- ✤ Your child enjoys time with you, discussing what they have learned, what they do not understand, and things they hear that concern them.

CHAPTER NINE

SCOUTING AMERICA—
STAR TO EAGLE

We must change boys from a "what can I get"
to a "what can I give" attitude.

— ROBERT BADEN-POWELL

Be Prepared . . . the meaning of the motto is that a Scout must
prepare himself by previous thinking out and practicing how to act
on any accident or emergency so that he is never taken by surprise.

— ROBERT BADEN-POWELL

One version of the Star Scout[38] text for courts of honor reads:

---

38. SCOUTING AMERICA: Star to Eagle, Venturing, Sea Scouts; Ages ~12–18 years; GIRL
SCOUTS: Senior, Ambassador; TRAIL LIFE: Adventurer; SCOUTS: Explorer; GUIDES: Ranger;
AMERICAN HERITAGE GIRLS: Pioneer, Patriot.

> Whether or not you realize it, by meeting your Star Scout requirements, you have left the group of those who receive Scouting. Tonight, you will join a smaller and more significant group—those whose duty and privilege it is to give Scouting to others. As you receive your Star Scout badge, it must be with full realization that you accept with that badge the giving of leadership, guidance, and inspiration to younger Scouts.

Scouting discussions with your child should be more peer-to-peer. Support each other during meetings. As an assistant Scoutmaster, Scoutmaster, troop committee member, merit badge counselor, or in another support role, model servant leadership. Your Scout might ask you to work with a youth who is trying to complete a merit badge or rank advancement, or you might ask the same of your Scout. Relish shared and mutually delegated leadership with your child. Enjoy this rich season in your lives as you continue to prepare your child for his or her post-secondary-education world.

How your child fulfills their position of responsibility reflects your training. Servant leadership should be evident in Star, Life, and Eagle Scouts. Your son or daughter is now a "Big Scout"—the kind who intimidated their younger self. Reinforce their role as a helper to and protector of younger Scouts. In their leadership positions, Scouts learn to make, and live by, their decisions with the guidance of the Scoutmaster and assistant Scoutmaster(s).

Your teen needs you to empower them to make informed decisions outside of Scouts, within the framework of rules you establish and enforce for your family. Decision-making knowledge is of little value without the opportunity to use it. Scouting will add strain to your relationship if adult and youth Scout leaders trust your Scout to make informed decisions for the unit but, in contrast, he or she lives a tightly controlled life with no autonomy at home. Your maturing child needs to learn and practice how to be an adult with you available to counsel, support, and, if necessary, rescue them. It is difficult to maintain balance, but a balance you must find.

Scouts can help your child refine their decision-making and leadership skills. Encourage your Scout to attend a National Youth Leadership Training (NYLT) course, the pinnacle of youth leadership training. They will develop leadership skills on par with those taught in corporate executive training for a small fraction of the cost and a decade ahead of their peers. They will make new friends and connect with youth leaders from other units as they learn to fulfill their leadership roles more effectively. If you have completed your Wood Badge ticket, consider staffing an NYLT course.

Scouting will help you prepare your child to leave home either to attend post-secondary education[39] or join the workplace, but he or she needs you, their parent(s), at the center of their support system as they navigate the complexities of becoming an adult. You can approach these developmental years with fear and trepidation, or you can build a firm foundation and look forward to them. With the social and other challenges your child faces, you can either work through them together and be their hero, or avoid the awkward discussions, leave them to fend for themselves, and lose both their respect for you and the opportunity for a deep, rewarding relationship. It is not time for friendship yet. They need you to be their dad or mom, confident in your unconditional love.

During these middle- to late-teen years, youth are wired to look to peers to affirm their identity. The desire to fit in can overshadow your counsel or, worse, start down a path that destroys your relationship. "Parents play an essential role in preparing teens to navigate pressured— or even risky—situations."[40] You will largely determine if teenage years

---

39. Helen E. Johnson and Christine Schelhas-Miller, *Don't Tell Me What to Do, Just Send Money*, New York: St. Martins Griffin, 2000, 2011.

40. Taylor Tropea, "What Teens Think About Peer Pressure—And How Parents Can Help", Center for Parent and Teen Communication, Oct. 27, 2022, parentandteen.com/what-teens-think-peer-pressure.

are full of growth and mutual respect or disappointment and disrespect, whether you intend to or not. Carve out sacred quality time with your son or daughter to help them grow into an emotionally healthy teenager.

Become your child's scapegoat now if you have not yet. Peers' opinions continue to increase in value for your child. Let them save face and blame you. (See the previous chapter for additional details.)

Teen schedules: It is uncanny how your teenager is invariably ready to talk at the time least convenient for you. Late night seems to be a favorite chat time. Stay up, even if you are an "early to bed, early to rise" type. When you must defer a discussion—and that should be rarely—ask for a summary, then schedule time soon to continue. And keep that appointment! If the interruption is a crisis to your child (though it may not be to you), stop and listen. If you shut them down often enough, they may well shut you out for good.

Advancement: Merit Badges

Scouts earn most of their merit badges after completing First Class. Discourage your child from becoming a mere accumulator. Help them find their satisfaction in mastery, not box ticking.

As you peruse the merit badge requirements together, look for topics on which you are an expert or could develop the knowledge or skills to teach a merit badge. Troops and districts need merit badge counselors.

Merit badge work can open another door to enter your child's world. They might find a new hobby, discover that a current pastime could become a new merit badge on their sash, or even start down the path toward a career. Encourage them to use merit badges to expand their horizons, and discern their aptitudes, likes, and dislikes.

Give your Scout your focused attention as you scroll through the site[41] or flip through the Scouting America Requirements book together. Ask what they learn from the badges they work on, about the topic, and about themselves. Listen for what interests them and what they want to avoid. Use every avenue at your disposal to learn more about your Scout—and let them learn about you. Affirm who and how God made them. Your focus and affirmation will go beyond developing new skills. It will give your son or daughter the confidence to bring to you their struggles and crises.

Remember that this is *your Scout's* work. Completion must be up to them. Did they set a target number of badges to earn? You could confirm and, if their goal stands, encourage them, but do not make it your goal.

Some troops have a library of merit badge handbooks, but check the dates against the website! Expired handbooks still contain useful information, even if the requirements change, but Scouts must complete the current list. (Changes instituted after they start will not affect completion.) If the troop has severely out-of-date merit badge handbooks, or is missing the one your child wants to earn, consider buying one and donating it to the troop when your Scout finishes the badge.

After your Scout earns a merit badge, have them consider helping teach. The Roman philosopher Seneca said, "While we teach, we learn." Today, this is called the protégé effect.[42] Your child will deepen their understanding when they teach what they know. So will you. You might find a badge you could teach together.

---

41. Scouting America Merit Badge Hub, www.scouting.org/skills/merit-badges.

42. Annie Murphy Paul, "The Protégé Effect: Why Teaching Someone Else Is the Best Way to Learn," *Psychology Today*, June 13, 2012, www.psychologytoday.com/us/blog/how-to-be-brilliant/201206/the-protege-effect.

High Adventure and the Increasing Cost of Failure

Many units reserve high adventure trips (including Scouting America and other properties) to Scouts who have completed their First Class rank as these treks require greater skills, coordination, confidence, and maturity.

Do you love to canoe, hike, climb mountains, sail, or camp remotely? Then consider coordinating a trek for your child's troop—even if your Scout does not go. If you think the trek is something you would enjoy together, talk to your Scout before you sign up. He or she may need to get out from under your shadow to further develop their leadership skills.

With these grander adventures, the cost of failure increases dramatically. As you increase your teen's autonomy, some of their decisions will not be very good. Your home must be your Scout's refuge, where they can depend on your support and comfort as they work through mistakes and failures. Your child is learning how to be an adult, and I have yet to meet a perfect adult.

I do not mean to imply that failures do not have consequences (e.g., being grounded for breaking a family rule, having to earn money to repair a wrecked car, or even having to pass a night in jail for drinking). Your Scout needs to be able to rely on your unconditional love through such a trial.

Burnout and Competing Interests

Some Scouts burn out during this phase. Your child may have exhibited strong leadership since Cub Scouts and is ready for a break, or there are other activities they want to explore (a new sport, dance, band, theater, etc.). Discuss their long-term goals to help them see how Scouting could fit in. Some Scouts focus on sports or band in the fall, and may attend only one or two campouts, then emphasize Scouts in the spring and summer. Encourage your child; do not coerce them. Teach them how to weigh good competing options. Pros/cons lists, rank weighting their options, or other techniques may help.

Promote Scouts, even if your Scout cannot make it their primary extracurricular activity. If they once planned to reach their program's top rank or honor, find out if that is still their plan. Your child may need a different Scouting offering. Older Scouts can join a Venturing crew or Sea Scout ship and still become an Eagle Scout (if they earn their First Class rank in a troop).

If your Scout is interested in the outdoors, they could consider pursuing a Distinguished Conservation Service Award (called the William T. Hornaday Award prior to 2020), or the International Activities badge if they like to travel. Do the Scouting America high-adventure bases entice your Scout? Help them find the element of Scouting that keeps them engaged and where they can contribute to their troop, crew, or ship. Scouting has a program for almost everyone.

If your son or daughter reaches a point where they want to quit, your relationship should be strong enough for open, honest discussions. Ensure there is not a social dynamic, fear, or troop dysfunction that is pushing them away from Scouting. They may need some time away. You can hope that "Absence [will make] the heart grow fonder."[43] During their break, keep them informed about high adventure plans and help with Eagle projects together. Leave the door wide open to return.

CAUTION FOR PARENTS OF
SCOUTS APPROACHING EAGLE

Remember one of the first tenets of this book: Your child's goals must be *your child's* goals. Many parents push their children to earn Eagle

---

43. Adaption of a quote by first-century BC Roman poet Sextus Aurelius Propertius, according to www.phrases.org.uk/meanings/absence-makes-the-heart-grow-fonder.html.

before they start high school. (For a boy, this is often to "get it done before 'fumes' distract him—perfumes and car fumes.") With few exceptions, the rushed Scout misses the full benefit of the rank because they have not lived enough life or experienced sufficient leadership.

If *your child's* goal is to become an Eagle Scout, the troop will provide an advisor to help them, but they still need your support. Be available to brainstorm or connect them to your network, or listen to their frustrations. Ask questions that help them get to the answer they need. Ensure your Scout has a contingency plan to prepare for what could go wrong, or right. (This should be part of their project plan.) We volunteered for most other projects throughout my son's Scouting career, so he created a bolt-on activity (and budget) if he had more volunteers than his design required. This "sub-project" was something his school (his project's beneficiary) would like but did not expect to be completed. He needed that plan. His project required twenty-five people. Over one hundred showed up!

Offer help, but accept "none" as a sign of maturing independence, not rejection—and be ready for them to change their minds when you least expect it. Be their advocate as they pursue a goal that fewer than 0.3% of American youth achieve.

Do not push your child to fit into your timeline or because you worry they lack the stamina to reach "their" goals.

What if you panic? The deadline is approaching, so you shift from encouraging to pushing to manipulating your Scout. STOP. Ask questions. LISTEN. Is your Scout ready? Have their goals changed? Is something else happening in their world? Help them navigate life's challenges and prepare them to re-engage and finish, if that is what they decide.

What if they start but do not complete their Eagle rank? What if they only lack one or two requirements? Push them now, right? Wrong! Their relationship with you is more important. If your Scout stops short of the goal they once set, their "I will not make that mistake again" regret may become a powerful motivator later in life.

Scouts who reach their program's highest achievement only through your implementing restrictions/conditions ("You cannot get your driver's license, or have a later curfew, or date someone, or [fill in the blank] until you get your Eagle") or bribes ("If you earn your Eagle, we will buy you a car/pay for your college/give you more privileges . . .") learn that you lack confidence in them, that you value the rank more highly than they do, or that "their" Eagle is of greater worth to you than their desires. Do not do that to your child.

The Eagle Scout rank is a noble ambition. Challenge your son or daughter to strive toward it. Encourage them when they get distracted or discouraged, but only as you remember that "Advancement is simply a means to an end, not an end in itself."[44] Read the Scouting America Vision and Mission Statements, the Scout Oath, Scout Law, and Scout Motto. Not one mentions ranks or advancement.

A Scout who walks the Eagle path matures into a more informed citizen, better leader and follower, better employee and employer, better friend, and better woman or man. Experiential learning is the means to further Scouting America's primary desire for youth—personal growth. Do not miss your opportunity to shape that personal growth and grow with your Scout.

FRIENDSHIP WITH YOUR CHILD

Throughout this book, I have reiterated the message, "You are not your child's friend." Let me clarify. I do not mean you should not enjoy fun times together. I hope you do! You might share a hobby (Scouts!?!). What a blessing if your child embraces your instruction, advice, and correction.

44. Advancement and Awards, Scouting America, https://www.scouting.org/programs/scouts-bsa/advancement-and-awards/.

In the *Scout world*, you may be more peer than parent—indeed, you could be junior to the senior patrol leader living in your house.

Your collegiality must have limits, however. Your Scout is still a child who needs a parent, even if they tower over you when you stand together. Friendship might look inviting, but in a crisis, they need your decisive parental leadership. Your child's friends will come and go, causing varying degrees of pain. Their respect for you and confidence in your love for them must be deep enough to survive the decisions you need to make for their welfare and the rules you must enforce for their protection. A friend cannot fill that role.

For Fathers of Daughters

Dads, your daughter needs you in a humbling and unique way, different from a father–son, mother–daughter, or mother–son relationship. Build her up.

Here are a few quotes regarding the impact fathers have on their daughters:[45]

"When a daughter hears 'I love you' from her father, she feels complete."

"Keep your comments positive, keep them on these qualities, and you can't lose. Instead of saying, 'I love you because you're so beautiful,' tell her that you love her because there is no one else in the world like her." [Do not tie your love for her to her appearance, but to who she is as a person.]

"Men, good men: We need you. We—mothers, daughters, and sisters—need your help to raise healthy young women. We need every ounce of masculine courage and wit you own, because fathers, more than anyone else, set the course for a daughter's life."

---

45. Meg Seeker, *Strong Fathers, Strong Daughters: 10 Secrets Every Father Should Know*, Regnery Publishing, 2006, pp. 4, 5, 7, 8. Dr. Seeker has over twenty years' experience counseling girls.

FEARS AND CONCERNS

Your child's brave face could mask insecurities. Leadership development is one of the greatest benefits of Scouting, but a troop with excellent youth leaders can inadvertently create insecurity in your Scout, who might worry about measuring up. Reassure your Scout that the great leader they see today developed over time, just as they will. Help them to avoid comparison to anyone other than their best self.

Watch for changes in behavior or pulling back from Scouts. Ask good questions to learn what is happening in their world. Society targets older teens with lies about who they are and who they can become. Be your child's trusted source for truth. The past decade of building your relationship was for times like this.

Fear may creep into your psyche as well. Your child is growing up, about to fulfill what you have been preparing them to do—to leave your nest to establish their own. Avoid the temptation to become your child's friend. They need you to be their mom and dad now more than ever.

SAMPLE CONVERSATIONS

Unhelpful

Parent: "Why are you home so late? You know the rules."

Scout: "It's not my fault. My friend's car ran out of gas and my phone died."

Parent: "You need to plan ahead. I've told you over and over that you need to keep your phone charged. You also need to pick better friends who aren't too stupid to read a gas gauge."

Scout: "Whatever. I'm going to sleep." *Storms off and slams their bedroom door.*

Helpful

Parent: "You are home later than we agreed. I was worried about you because you honor your commitments and keep your word."

Scout: "I'm sorry. We changed our plans and decided to go to the beach, so I changed clothes in a hurry and left my backup charger in my other jeans. To make it more complicated, my friend's mom's car ran out of gas. We didn't realize the gas gauge didn't work. Their phone was also out of battery, so we had to walk back to their house."

Parent: "We can talk about who you met in the morning. You are a good problem solver. How might you avoid this happening again?"

Scout: "Can we go to the phone store and replace my battery? It doesn't last even a day. Also, since Jill doesn't have much extra money, will you buy them one of those phone chargers with different charging cables, since we have different kinds of phones?"

Parent: "Great solution. You are developing great problem-solving skills. Do you think they would split the cost with us?"

Scout: "I will give you their half. Thanks. I love you. I have homework, and then I need to sleep."

Hug each other before the Scout slips off to their room and eases their door closed to avoid waking younger siblings.

Unhelpful

Parent: "Why aren't you the senior patrol leader? You need to be the one leading the troop."

Scout: "I don't want to be the SPL. It's too much pressure."

Parent: "Then why are you even in Scouts?"

Scout: "I don't know. Maybe I should spend more time practicing soccer."

Parent: "Probably so. You need to get your goal count up so that you can get a college scholarship, and I won't have to spend all of my money on your school."

Scout: "Whatever."

Helpful

Parent: "Are you learning the leadership skills you hoped you would in Scouts?"

Scout: "I don't know. Maybe some."

Parent: "Will you help me to understand what you mean by that?"

Scout: "The current senior patrol leader is really dynamic and everyone loves them. I don't think I can measure up, and I don't want to disappoint the troop."

Parent: "I love your concern for the good of your troop. How many other leadership positions has the current SPL held?"

Scout: "Good point! They have been an assistant SPL, an instructor, they helped a Cub Scout pack as a den chief, and they might have been a chaplain aide. I guess they didn't become SPL overnight. I like helping the other Scouts, and they tell me I'm pretty good at all the First Class skills, so I think I might run for an instructor position in the next troop election."

Parent: "Your thought process has matured—the way you just considered how to apply the skills others have affirmed in you, to help the troop and grow as a leader. If you run for SPL one day, you will 'Be Prepared.' Pun intended." *Grins.*

Scout: "You and your puns. But thank you for your confidence in me."

Unhelpful

Parent: "You'll be fifteen next summer. You need to finish your Eagle before we let you get your license. Let's get started. Who do I need to call?"

Scout: "There's an Eagle coach in our troop, but I think I'm the one who's supposed to talk to them."

Parent: "Talk to them at the next troop meeting, and then I'll call them to get everything sorted out."

Scout: "Yes, sir."

Helpful

Parent: "I overheard some of the other Scouts talking about their Eagle Scout projects. Is earning Eagle still one of your goals?"

Scout: "Absolutely! One of the Scouts in my patrol is already working on theirs, but their parents are stressing them out over it."

Parent: "I'm sorry to hear that. You have time, but I encourage you to map it out so that it doesn't sneak up on you."

Scout: "That sounds like a good idea. Will you help me make a schedule? I want to improve my leadership and enjoy the experience as well."

Parent: "Wow. I wish I had been as wise and mature when I was your age! I rushed through my Eagle Scout and since regretted it. Of course I will help you, but is there anyone else in the troop who could help you? I made too many mistakes, so I might not be your best advisor."

Scout: "Thanks for the reminder. We have an Eagle Scout coach. I'll ask them. Thank you!"

Parent: "We're proud of you and love watching you growing into an amazing adult. You live the Scout Oath and Law. Whether you earn your Eagle Scout rank or don't is up to you. Neither will change how much we love you. We're ready to help you when you ask."

Scout: "I really appreciate your confidence in me. I love you."

RECAP

SCOUTING AMERICA—STAR TO EAGLE

Parenting

- Continue to enter your child's changing and confusing world. It is confusing to them as well.

- Support and encourage work toward Eagle, but do not bribe, badger, or threaten.

- Listen more than you speak. Ask open-ended questions.

- Help your child process and overcome their fears of leadership, of growing up, of becoming independent.

- Move toward a peer relationship in your Scouting world.

  - Avoid the temptation to become your child's friend.

  - Your role as your child's parent is more important than ever.

- You help other Scouts more than your own at meetings and on campouts.

- Now more than ever, your home must be a safe place to fail; the cost of failure will increase.

- Coach by reviewing plays at home.

SCOUTING

- Scouts earn most of their merit badges after earning their First Class rank.

- High adventure treks are generally open to Scouts after they complete First Class.

- Scouting is a safe place to fail.

- Teach parents of new Scouts how to navigate your troop. Model servant leadership.

- Debrief with your Scout after troop meetings and campouts.

- Attend troop committee meetings and district or council roundtables.

- Get trained!

SIGNS OF SUCCESS

- You and your Scout hold leadership positions.

- Your child seeks your guidance to navigate uncomfortable situations.

- Your child looks for ways to help others and challenges their peers to do the same.

- Other Scouts seek their help or advice.

- Your Scout is far more independent in setting and working toward their goals.

- Your Scout exhibits servant leadership inside and outside of Scouts.

- Adults ask to do their boards of review.

- Through work on a diverse array of merit badges, whether or not they finish, your Scout discovers or affirms interests and passions.

- Your Scout is an asset to the troop.

CHAPTER TEN

DUTY TO GOD

Trust should be the basis for all our moral training.

— ROBERT BADEN-POWELL

No man is much good unless he believes in God and obeys His laws. So every Scout should have a religion.

— ROBERT BADEN-POWELL

Scouting[46] expects participants to have a relationship with God. You should be your child's primary religious leader—you understand their character, challenges, temptations, and joys better than any pastor, rabbi, priest, or other religious leader or teacher. Help your Scout further their duty to God and their relationship with God. Encourage multi-faith conversations, not to diminish theirs as one of many, but to strengthen it through understanding how and why their beliefs differ. Genuine toler-

---

46. SCOUTING AMERICA: All ranks; All Ages; GIRL SCOUTS: My Promise, My Faith; TRAIL LIFE: Part of core program; SCOUTS: Faith Activity Badges; GUIDES: None; AMERICAN HERITAGE GIRLS: Part of core program.

ance—accepting others without necessarily agreeing with their ideas—will equip your Scout to engage in healthy, respectful religious dialogue.

Every rank from Tiger to Eagle (including Eagle Palms) requires the Scout to describe how they have done their "duty to God." For a Cub Scout, a representative requirement is: "Discuss with your parent, guardian, den leader, or other caring adult what it means to do your duty to God. Tell how you do your duty to God in your daily life."[47] For Scouting America, the requirement for every rank includes some element of: "Tell how you have done your duty to God and how you have lived the Scout Oath and Scout Law in your everyday life."[48]

Scouts partners with other organizations to provide ready-made, age-appropriate programs to teach your child and their unit beliefs that are foundational to your faith. Your Scout can wear emblems of completion for any faith's "Duty to God" curriculum on their uniform.

Scouting America troops further demonstrate their commitment to this principle through faith-based leadership roles. Chaplain aide satisfies the position of responsibility requirement for Star, Life, and Eagle ranks. This Scout works with the adult chaplain to conduct "Scout's Own" services on campouts.[49] That is the most visible aspect of the position, and one that helps develop organizational skills, public speaking, and compassion, but they are also expected to "encourage troop members to strengthen their own relationships with God through personal prayer and devotion and participation in religious activities appropriate to their faith."[50]

Our son's term as chaplain aide helped prepare him for a career that requires him to preach and teach. A decade later, he continues to hone the skills he began as a Scout.

---

47. *Bear Handbook*, p. 74.

48. *Scouts BSA Handbook*, p. 450.

49. The BSA chaplain, U.S. Scouting Service Project, www.usscouts.org/chaplain/scout-sown.asp.

50. Manual for Chaplains and Chaplain Aides, BSA, www.scouting.org/programs/scouts-bsa/troop-resources/troop-chaplain-and-chaplain-aide-roles/manual-for-chaplains-and-chaplain-aides.

Scouting America provides an additional tool for older Scouts called "ethical controversies" to investigate their convictions.[51] Developed for Venturing crews, these guided discussions provide thought-provoking scenarios to generate deeper conversations. Use them with your child and other Scouts to help them understand what *they* believe, and create an opportunity to discuss how their faith can help answer the dilemmas presented.

RELIGIOUS EMBLEMS

"The Religious Emblems programs are developed by the national religious organizations to encourage their members to grow stronger in their faith. The Scouting agencies have approved of these programs and allow the awards to be worn on the official uniforms, but the emblems are created and administered by the various religious groups."[52] These programs encompass most of the major world religions. As a Christian, I am most familiar with those created by Programs of Religious Activities with Youth (P.R.A.Y.), which "upholds duty to God by . . . encouraging churches to embrace Scouting as ministry; i.e., Faith-Based Initiative (FBI)."[53]

P.R.A.Y. and related organizations provide you with ready-made resources aligned with Scouting to teach God's standard of right and wrong and encourage your Scout to live up to that standard. I led all four of the P.R.A.Y. Protestant programs with my son's pack, then troop, and facilitated a co-ed discussion using the God and Life curriculum for my daughter's Venturing crew. This facet of Scouting provided me with a way to grow closer to my children, know their friends and parents on a spiritual level, and deepen my faith. We questioned and learned together.

51. Ethical Controversies: Vignettes, Scouting.org, adapted from *Creative Conflict*, by D.W. Johnson and R.T. Johnson, Interaction Book Company, Minneapolis, Minnesota, 1987, www.scouting.org/wp-content/uploads/2019/04/ethical_controversies_vignettes.pdf.

52. Religious Emblems, Programs of Religious Activities with Youth (P.R.A.Y.), www.praypub.org/religious-emblems.

53. P.R.A.Y. Partner Boy Scouts of America, Programs of Religious Activities with Youth (P.R.A.Y.), www.praypub.org/bsa.

Your Child's Faith

Your son or daughter must own their faith—it must be *their* faith. This becomes increasingly important as your child prepares to move out of your house to pursue post-secondary education or employment. I believe that "good, church-going kids" walk away from their faith after leaving home for one of two reasons.

First, that child's faith was never their own. Parents took the family to services through bribes or autocratic rule and did not allow questions that could develop faith. They did not prepare their child for the pressure of a secular society that may undermine what your family espouses.

Second, some children were raised by overly zealous parents who enforced rigid rules with no opportunity for discussion. These parents rewarded "right" behavior and punished infractions swiftly and sometimes severely. They did not teach their children how to make informed decisions in a loving environment with clear boundaries, only how to obey rules imposed on them. Appearance trumped the heart. Without rules to protect them, the child must now make decisions their parents did not train them to make, often with dire results.

Study the tenets of your faith together, using duty to God resources, your faith's membership process, statement of faith, catechism, or other program. Guide your child to develop their faith, as you refine yours. A firm foundation of faith is one of the greatest gifts you can give your child.

Fears and Concerns

A Scout may fear questioning their faith. (Adults might also!) Your younger Scout will follow your lead, but your older Scout must refine their faith. Invite their questions. Make them feel comfortable investigating what they believe—and why.

Are you afraid your child will ask you something that you cannot answer? Great! Share that fear! Offer to join your scout in a conversation with your religious leader, invite your religious leader to your home for a meal so that the whole family can participate (as appropriate), or look for answers in your religion's holy book(s). Your honesty in admitting the limits of your knowledge frees your child to be genuine with their struggles. Deepen your faith together.

Do not overreact if your child strays. Did you? Sharing your past or present doubts and missteps does not make you weak; it makes you real. Share why you believe what you believe and how you got there. If your son or daughter strays from your family's faith, do not let them stray uninformed. Express your concerns through dialogue, not diatribe, as you pray for their return.

SAMPLE CONVERSATIONS

Unhelpful (Older Scout)

Scout:	"Can I ask you some questions about God?"
Parent:	"What do you mean, 'questions about God'? You cannot question God or you will not be welcome in services."
Scout:	"But I don't understand some things."
Parent:	"Then you need to read the Statement of Belief. It will tell you what you are supposed to believe."
Scout:	"Okay."

Helpful (Older Scout)

Scout:	"Can I ask you some questions about God?"
Parent:	"Of course! I wish I had asked more questions about my faith when I was your age. Do you mind if I share a

	short story about what happened to me in college? Will you remember your questions? They are important to me."
Scout:	"I wrote them down. I like your college stories, or some of them anyway."

Both smile.

Parent:	"I used to go to church all the time with my family, but no one would let us question our faith—not my parents, not our pastor, not my teachers. When I got to college, and my parents no longer made me go to church, I lost my faith for many years. I let other things take my attention. After we got married, we started going back to church. I missed years where my faith could have developed. I'm proud of you working to understand what you believe and not accepting our faith without questions. You are mature for your age, and I enjoy learning with you and from you."
Scout:	"Thanks. I want to be strong in my faith. My friend's sister went crazy when she got to college. She was a perfect student in high school but flunked out of college and had some terrible boyfriends. She's still trying to correct her mistakes. I do not want to ruin my life."
Parent:	"We don't want you to go through any unnecessary pain either. You are wiser than your years to prepare yourself to thrive in college academically, emotionally, and spiritually. If we don't know the answers to your questions, you could schedule time with the pastor. He understands our faith better than I do. Then, we will all learn. What questions do you have?"

Scout: "Well, first, why ..."

Family spends the next few hours looking for answers to their questions and sets up a time to meet with their pastor.

The Role of Faith in Scouting

On my honor I will do my best to do my duty to God and my country ...

> — First part of the Scout Oath

We, the members of Girl Scouts of the United States of America, [are] united by a belief in God ...

> — Preamble, Constitution of Girl Scouts of the United States of America[54]

Our Mission is to guide generations of courageous young men to honor God, lead with integrity, serve others, and experience outdoor adventure.

> — Mission Statement, Trail Life USA

Building women of integrity through service to God, family, community, and country.

> — Mission Statement, American Heritage Girls[55]

54. Blue Book of Basic Documents, 2023, Girl Scouts, www.girlscouts.org/content/dam/girlscouts-gsusa/forms-and-documents/about-girl-scouts/facts/GSUSA_BlueBook.pdf.

55. American Heritage Girls (AGH), americanheritagegirls.org/about-ahg.

The Boy Scouts of America maintains that no member can grow into the best kind of citizen without recognizing an obligation to God and, therefore, recognizes the religious element in the training of the member, but it is absolutely nonsectarian in its attitude toward that religious training. Its policy is that the home and organization or group with which a member is connected shall give definite attention to religious life. Only persons willing to subscribe to this Declaration of Religious Principle and to the Bylaws of the Boy Scouts of America shall be entitled to certificates of membership.

– BSA DECLARATION OF RELIGIOUS PRINCIPLE[56]

A Scout is . . . Reverent.

– SCOUT LAW

---

56. Manual for Chaplains and Chaplain Aides, BSA, www.scouting.org/programs/scouts-bsa/troop-resources/troop-chaplain-and-chaplain-aide-roles/manual-for-chaplains-and-chap-lain-aides.

RECAP

DUTY TO GOD

Parenting

- Enter the world of your child's faith as it grows and develops throughout Scouting.

- Encourage questions about faith and be the safest place for your Scout to ask them.

- Prepare your son or daughter to take *their* faith with them into post-secondary education and/or the workplace.

- Share with your child what you believe, and why, in greater depth as they mature.

- Do not panic if your older Scout begins to doubt the religion of their youth. Work together to answer their questions.

Scouting

- Every rank, from Tiger to Eagle, including Eagle Palms, requires the Scout to describe how they have fulfilled their "duty to God."

- Ask your older Scout to share how they have fulfilled their "duty to God" requirement prior to a Board of Review.

  - They are thinking about it, so you are not asking for any incremental effort.

  - Listen and discuss. Do not tell them what to say. The answers must belong to your Scout.

  - Help them navigate what they believe. Be prepared for societal messaging to undermine your teaching.

- Campouts should include a "Scout's Own" service.

- Scouts and adults can earn religious emblems to wear on their uniforms.

- Scouts BSA has religious leadership opportunities for Scouts (chaplain aide) and adults (chaplain).

- Use Venturing ethical controversies with older Scouts.

Signs of Success

- Your child wants to attend worship services with your family.

- Your Scout wants to earn the religious emblem for their age.

- Your older Scout asks challenging questions about their faith. They wrestle with beliefs but seek your counsel.

- You and your older Scout seek answers independently, together, and as a family. All of you seek input from your religious leaders.

- Your Scout regularly reads the holy book(s) of your faith. So do you.

- You are open to any question about your faith, and your child knows you will answer honestly, without chastisement or panic.

CHAPTER 11

PARTING THOUGHTS

*Encourage and support your kids, because children
are apt to live up to what you believe of them.*

– LADY BIRD JOHNSON

Loyalty is a feature in a boy's character that inspires boundless hope.

– ROBERT BADEN-POWELL

"Now, by virtue of the authority vested in me by the National Council of Scouting America, I hereby award the rank of Eagle Scout to [your child's name]."

What Scouting America parent does not hope to hear those words at their Scout's Eagle court of honor? Scouting programs offer unmatched breadth and depth in outdoor and life skills training, citizenship instruction, teamwork development, and developing effective communicators. With your guidance and support, your child will set and reach goals they would unlikely even consider were it not for Scouts.

Scouting has improved the lives of over 500 million youth worldwide since 1907. Sadly, today only about 0.6% of American youth participate in this life-changing opportunity, though there are more than 50 million youth and adults involved in Scouting worldwide. Your Scout is part of an elite group and joins a rich legacy.

Your children who do not participate in Scouts can still benefit from the aims and methods Scouting embodies. Ask your Scout to teach your family the skills they learn. Camp in the backyard or build a fire pit and cook over the open fire. Enjoy fun together while you all learn beneficial skills.

Be Your Child's Chronicler

Young children have no idea what they will need in ten minutes, let alone ten years. The teenage brain is so distracted that the best laid plans are often set aside. Create physical and electronic repositories for advancement records, awards, patches, souvenirs from special activities, photos, cards, and notes. Your Scout will be grateful for your treasure trove and data repository when they apply for college or a job.

Attend Eagle Scout courts of honor when your child starts Cub Scouts to provide a vision for their Scouting future and give you ideas for what to save for your Scout's event, should that day come. If it does not, enjoy your box of memories with your former Scout and, maybe, your "grand Scout."

Data and tangible reminders are not the only reason to store these items. C. S. Lewis wrote, "A pleasure is full grown only when it is remembered."[57] It is not just fun to reminisce. It enriches the original experience!

---

57. C.S. Lewis, *Out of the Silent Planet*, New York, HarperOne, 2012, Kindle version, p. 75.

Pick Your Battles

You can avoid much parenting consternation with good positioning. Provide options from which to pick rather than restrictions. Save the restrictions for health and safety needs to the extent possible. Baden-Powell understood this: "The boy is not governed by 'don't,' but is led by 'do.'"

Your child desires and needs some control over their life, so provide it in ways acceptable to you. With your young child, replace "Do this/eat this/wear this" with "Which of these do you prefer to do/eat/wear?" Do not offer open-ended options, which can lead to unnecessary frustration for you both. Provide the options, but offer your child genuine choice.

As your child matures, you must increase their autonomy. Your older teen needs to learn how to govern themselves under your protection. That child will want or demand full autonomy. They are not ready for that, so strike a balance through frank, honest, and loving discussion. This is not a negotiation among equals. Be the parent.

Do not establish a consequence for disobedience that you will not enforce. Say what you mean, and mean what you say.[58] Children thrive with reasonable boundaries, which must expand as they grow older and demonstrate increased maturity.[59]

---

58. Based on Lewis Carroll's book, *Alice's Adventures in Wonderland*.

59. Katherine Lee, "How to Set Healthy Boundaries for Kids," *verywell family*, April 21, 2021, www.verywellfamily.com/whos-the-boss-how-to-set-healthy-boundaries-for-kids-3956403.

Be the Best Parent You Can Be

Scouting will help you raise your child to become a healthy, well-adjusted adult. If you do everything you are "supposed to do" and your child is a model Scout, you still have no guarantee that they will be free from emotional or behavioral problems, though the probability is much lower.[60] Success in Scouting does not guarantee a shining future.

If you combine the training provided through Scouts and your religious institution's teaching with the advice in this book, you will decrease the probability and severity of teenage angst, your student will be more likely to experience fewer and less severe college crises, and you will increase the likelihood of enjoying a mutually rewarding relationship with your child throughout their life.

You have probably heard or read some variation of the quote "Character [or values, or faith] is more caught than taught." The truth is, your child needs both methods.[61] Teach your son or daughter by word and example.

We loved our children's teenage years and treasure the relationships we have with our adult children and their spouses. You can too! Be the servant leader your family needs you to be.

Want to Know More?

Are there conversations you wish I had included? Do you have questions you would like me to answer? Visit www.dharakalauthor.org and send me a message from the *Parenting Through the Ranks* page, or e-mail me at dharakalauthor@gmail.com.

---

60. University of South Australia, "Happy childhood? That's no guarantee for good mental health," *ScienceDaily*, 7 February 2021, www.sciencedaily.com/releases/2021/02/210207100710.htm.

61. Alison Hunt, "Taught or Caught? Experiences of Year 3 Students in a Uniting Church School," *International Educational Journal*, 2004, files.eric.ed.gov/fulltext/EJ903815.pdf.

ADDITIONAL RESOURCES

*My heroes are and were my parents. I can't see
having anyone else as my heroes.*

– MICHAEL JORDAN

It is easier to build strong boys than to repair broken men.

– FREDERICK DOUGLASS, 1855

My parenting was the culmination of mistakes I made, attempts to avoid the mistakes I saw others make, my desire to emulate good parenting evidenced by respectful children I observed, and reading parenting books. Lots of parenting books. Most of the resources I recommend reflect a Christian worldview because that is what I read, and I only recommend those I have read.

There are certainly other excellent resources, but I have not read them (or have forgotten them). Below are those I most recommend and why. If you have books to recommend, e-mail me along with why you like them, and I will consider adding them to the list of resources at www.dharakalauthor.org.

General Parenting

Parenting: The 14 Gospel Principles That Can Radically Change Your Family by Paul David Tripp. If I could read only one parenting book, it would be this one. It is not a "how-to" book; instead, it establishes principles, the "big picture."

Parenting Isn't for Cowards: The "You Can Do It" Guide for Hassled Parents by James Dobson, an excellent resource that uses research data to discuss children's innate natures and how to parent them.

How to Talk So Kids Will Listen & Listen So Kids Will Talk by Adele Faber and Elaine Mazlish, especially good when your child begins middle school.

Don't Tell Me What to Do, Just Send Money: The Essential Parenting Guide to the College Years by Helen Johnson and Christine Schelhas-Miller. I recommend that you read this during your child's senior year of high school. You may not want to believe some of the things in the book are possible, but they are.

A Method for Dating: Because Dating Happens . . . and It Doesn't Have to Be Horrible by Matt Lantz, an excellent online resource for shepherding your child through dating.

Pornography: Fighting for Purity (31-Day Devotionals for Life) by Deepak Reju. Pornography is rampant among teens (and adults). This is a 31-day devotional to help stop the cycle. Follow up with *Rescue Plan* and *Rescue Skills* listed below.

Rescue Plan: Charting a Course to Restore Prisoners of Pornography by Deepak Reju and Jonathan Holmes. This is written for the person walking with someone struggling with pornography; use in combination with *Rescue Skills* below.

Rescue Skills: Essential Skills for Restoring the Sexually Broken by Deepak Reju and Jonathan Holmes. An excellent resource to help if your child struggles with pornography and is meant to be read with your child.

Raising Sons

Bringing Up Boys: Practical Advice and Encouragement for Those Shaping the Next Generation of Men by James Dobson. Dobson had a son and a daughter as I do. Raising boys is different than raising girls. This book focuses on the unique elements of parenting sons.

Raising a Modern-Day Knight: A Father's Role in Guiding His Son to Authentic Manhood by Robert Lewis. I used this as a foundation for a father-and-son "Becoming a Man" retreat; it has suggestions for ceremonies to mark milestone transitions.

Raising Daughters

Secret Keeper Girl: The Power of Modesty for Tweens by Dannah Gresh. This and the next book are particularly helpful for mothers teaching daughters about modesty and self-esteem.

Secret Keeper: The Delicate Power of Modesty by Dannah Gresh. Same as above, but this one is geared toward older girls.

Strong Fathers, Strong Daughters: 10 Secrets Every Father Should Know by Meg Seeker. I wish I had read this book when my daughter was a teenager, but I only recently discovered it. This is the best book I have read for fathers raising daughters. It was made into a movie in 2022.

Queen Bees and Wannabes: Helping Your Daughter Survive Cliques, Gossip, Boys, and the New Realities of Girl World by Rosalind Wiseman. This is an eye-opening book into the world of teen girls and was the inspiration for the movie *Mean Girls*.

NAVIGATING THE SCOUTING AMERICA PROGRAM

The Unofficial Parent Handbook: A Compendium of Practical Information on Scouts BSA for Scout Parents by David Howell. This is the best resource I have found for understanding Scouting America program elements.

Scouts BSA Requirements (current year) by Scouting America. This book can help you grow closer to your Scout. Look through rank requirements and merit badge options to learn about your child's passions and dislikes, where they are confident or where they struggle (or will). Rank-specific *Handbooks* and *Leader's Guides* will offer similar opportunities for Cub Scouts. *Leader's Guides* are not restricted to leaders.

QUESTIONS TO ASK A PROSPECTIVE CUB SCOUT PACK

- ❖ Where do most of these children go to school? (For Cubs, same-school affiliation can be a great benefit. For our son, it was a way for friends from preschool to maintain their friendship after moving to different elementary schools.)

- ❖ How often do you camp? Do you camp in state parks or use Scout facilities? (Scout facilities tend to be safer because of better access control. And if they avoid Scout-owned properties, this may indicate animosity with the broader Scouting community.)

- ❖ What percentage of Scout parents are involved in the pack?

- ❖ Do you have parent training for parents of new Cub Scouts?

- ❖ When does the pack committee meet?

- ❖ Which troops do most of your Scouts join after Cub Scouts? (Visit them to make sure they support your family's values. You and your Scout are likely to end up there if you join this pack!)

- ❖ How active is your pack in district and council activities? (Packs with limited interaction in the larger organization can be a red flag and limit your Scout's opportunities.)

❖ How much are dues and camping or other fees? Are there scholarships available? (A uniform and books are expensive, and that is before camping fees, etc. If this is a financial burden for you, find a pack that has scholarships or a program that fits your budget.)

❖ What does the pack do for fundraising? Do all the Scouts join in? (Fundraising is a good way for your Scout to contribute to the pack. You may hear about Friends of Scouting, which raises funds for Scouting at the district and council levels. If your pack does not participate, this could indicate friction with the district or council.)

QUESTIONS TO ASK A PROSPECTIVE SCOUTING AMERICA TROOP, VENTURING CREW, OR SEA SCOUT SHIP

✤ Is your troop Scout-led? (Most will say yes. Watch during the meeting setup period to see whether it is the Scouts or the adults who give most of the direction. Actions speak louder than words.)

✤ Is there a Scout-to-First-Class program? How do you measure how well the Scouts learn the skills?

✤ Is the troop active with the district and council? (Some troops avoid district and council events, which will reduce networking and leadership development opportunities for you and your Scout.)

✤ What percentage of Scout parents are involved in the troop?

✤ Does the troop encourage Scouts to get their Eagle rank before or during high school? Is there a minimum age the troop recommends for a Scout to earn the First Class or Eagle Scout rank? (Beware of Eagle mills that focus on rushing Scouts through the program to post "impressive" statistics. Do not accept the "Scouts need to earn Eagle before the distractions of high school" position.)

✤ What kinds of high adventure activities does the troop do? Are there any troop-specific requirements to attend?

✤ Is there a healthy *esprit de corps* in patrols? Do patrols compete against each other in a way that creates humble winners and gracious losers? (Some units do not allow competition, which robs children of a natural motivator.)

✤ What is your camping style? Do all the Scouts use the same kind of tent? Are tents supplied by the troop?

✤ How much are dues and camping or other fees? Are there scholarships or other financial aid options available?

✤ What does the troop do for fundraising? Do all the Scouts participate? (You may hear about Friends of Scouting, which raises funds for Scouting at the district and council levels. If your pack does not participate, this could indicate friction with the district or council.)

✤ Observe. Do Scouts work together to solve problems? Do younger Scouts go to older Scouts, or do they go to the adults for most or all of their solutions? Either of the first two are good. If adults are the problem solvers, there is a problem in the leadership structure.

ABOUT THE AUTHOR

David Harakal has held pack, troop, crew, district, and council leadership roles, developed unit and district parent training materials, and created and taught parenting programs outside of Scouting. He was awarded the Scouting America Silver Beaver and Vale la Pena awards plus three President's Volunteer Service Awards. Harakal and his wife have two grown, married children, one an Eagle Scout and Order of the Arrow Vigil Honor member, and the other a past Venturing crew president.

NOTES

NOTES